Men-at-Arms • 446

The Confederate Army 1861–65 (6)

Missouri, Kentucky & Maryland

Ron Field • Illustrated by Richard Hook

Series editor Martin Windrow

First published in Great Britain in 2008 by Osprey Publishing
Midland House, West Way, Botley, Oxford OX2 0PH, UK
443 Park Avenue South, New York, NY 10016, USA

ISBN: 978 1 84603 188 5

Edited by Martin Windrow
Page layout: Alan Hamp
Index by Glyn Sutcliffe
Typeset in New Baskerville and Helvetica
Originated by PPS Grasmere Ltd
Printed in China through Worldprint

08 09 10 11 12   10 9 8 7 6 5 4 3 2 1

A CIP catalog record for this book is available from the British Library

FOR A CATALOG OF ALL BOOKS PUBLISHED BY
OSPREY MILITARY AND AVIATION PLEASE CONTACT:
North America
Osprey Direct, c/o Random House Distribution Center, 400 Hahn Road, Westminster, MD 21157
E-mail: info@ospreydirect.com

All other regions
Osprey Direct UK, P.O. Box 140 Wellingborough, Northants, NN8 2FA, UK
E-mail: info@ospreydirect.co.uk

Osprey Publishing is supporting the Woodland Trust, the UK's leading woodland conservation charity, by funding the dedication of trees.

www.ospreypublishing.com

Author's note

This title completes a sequence of books within the Men-at-Arms series providing a state-by-state analysis of the uniforms, arms and equipage worn and carried by the Militia and Volunteers who served the Confederate States during the American Civil War, 1861–65. Each of the 14 states that provided soldiers for the Southern cause is dealt with in order of secession, i.e. the order in which they left the Union. This arrangement helps to illustrate how some of the original seven Confederate States of America, formed on February 8, 1861, influenced the military fashion, and supply of weapons and equipment, of those states that later joined the Confederacy. The five previous titles in the sequence are listed on the inside rear cover of this book.

Acknowledgments

The author wishes to thank the following for their generous assistance: Clifton P. Hyatt, US Army Military History Institute, Carlisle, PA; Peter Harrington, Curator, Anne S. K. Brown Military Collection, Brown University, RI; Ara Kaye, Senior Reference Specialist, Newspaper Library, State Historical Society of Missouri, Columbia, MO; Connie Langum, Historian, Wilson's Creek National Battlefield, MO; Charlene Smith, Archivist, & Kevin Johnson, Collections Imaging Specialist, Kentucky Historical Society; Marie Dale, Preservation Reformatting Center, King Library South, University of Kentucky, Lexington; Kelly Betts, Assistant Curator of Manuscripts, Special Collections & Archives, Milton S. Eisenhower Library, Johns Hopkins University, Baltimore, MD; Jason Flahardy, Audio Visual Archives, University of Kentucky Libraries, Lexington; J. Dale West, Myron W. Gwimmer, Dave Mark, William Dunniway, John Sickles, James E. McGhee, Mark Jaegar, Bill Fannin, Peter Milne, Geoff Walden, and Alan Thrower.

Editor's note

Throughout this sequence of books, which draws heavily upon direct quotation from 19th-century texts, the changes in spelling conventions since that time produce unavoidable inconsistencies, which we hope are not too distracting. It was felt important to reproduce period quotations verbatim, but since the narrative text is in present-day American spelling the reader will often encounter – in the most obvious examples – both "grey" and "gray," "sabres" and "sabers."

Artist's note

Readers may care to note that the original paintings from which the color plates in this book were prepared are available for private sale. All reproduction copyright whatsoever is retained by the Publishers. All inquiries should be addressed to:

Richard Hook
P.O. Box 475, Hailsham, East Sussex BN27 2SL, UK

The Publishers regret that they can enter into no correspondence upon this matter.

THE CONFEDERATE ARMY 1861–65 (6) MISSOURI, KENTUCKY & MARYLAND

MISSOURI

ON MARCH 4, 1861, a secessionist flag was flown from the Berthold Mansion, the headquarters for the pro-Southern Minute Men in St Louis, Missouri. When a large crowd of armed pro-Union supporters attempted to tear it down, the Minute Men prepared to defend themselves with a "swivel gun" artillery piece, muskets and revolvers. The city police were called out to maintain the peace, and were reinforced by elements of citizen soldiery under BrigGen Daniel M. Frost, commander of the St Louis District of the Missouri Militia.

Although opposed to rebellion at that time, many members of the local militia – such as the St Louis Grays, Emmet Guards and Washington Blues – later joined forces with the Confederacy to fight for Southern Rights. The Independent Guards and a re-organized company of the Engineer Corps of National Guards had formed the

2nd Missouri Volunteer Militia under Col John S. Bowen by April of that year. Many others enlisted in the Missouri State Guard, and fought bravely under Sterling Price until the winter of 1861/62, when they were reorganized as volunteers into Confederate service, forming the First and Second Missouri brigades. Besides providing 62 State Guard units organized into eight separate divisions, a total of 48 cavalry, 9 artillery, and 37 infantry units from Missouri served the Confederacy, and distinguished themselves at actions including Wilson's Creek, Franklin, and the siege of Vicksburg.

Volunteer militia

As a border state, Missouri was sharply divided by the events which led to civil war in 1861.

John S. Bowen was active in the Missouri militia before the Civil War. Acting chief-of-staff to Gen Daniel M. Frost when Camp Jackson was attacked on May 10, 1861, he was commissioned colonel of the 2nd Missouri Volunteer Militia, and commanded the 1st Missouri Volunteer Infantry upon entering Confederate service. He wears the dark blue full dress uniform of a captain of the Missouri militia, which in turn appears to have been based on US Army regulations for 1857, complete with "dead-and-bright" gold bullion epaulettes. Note, however, the very deep cuffs, which were not a feature of regular army officers' uniforms. (Library of Congress)

Although admitted to the Union as a slave state in 1821, its population had been swelled by a strong body of antislavery settlers of German origin, who had congregated in or near St Louis by 1850. On the eve of the Civil War the old enrolled militia system of Missouri had been all but abandoned, and the sole military force in the state consisted of uniformed volunteer militia companies, the majority of which resided in St Louis, St Joseph and Jefferson City, the state capital. An act of the state legislature in 1859 authorized these companies – some of which were organized into regiments and battalions along the lines of the defunct enrolled militia – to choose their own uniforms, and for general officers to do likewise. For example, the West Point Grays were organized in Bates County during January 1860, and adopted "a becoming style of uniform" to be made of either "Southern or English manufactured goods," according to a report in the local press. The Stewartsville Rifles of St Joseph wore uniforms of "fine blue broadcloth" which included tight-fitting frock coats fastened with "eagle" buttons. The Missouri Light Artillery, of St Louis, chose a blue frock coat with red collar and cuffs edged with gold lace, brass shoulder scales, sky-blue pants with double red seam stripes, and a sky-blue felt cap with patent leather top, brass flaming shell device and red horsehair plume hanging on the right side.

The dress chosen by some antebellum companies may have been influenced by the uniforms of their grandfathers, as prescribed by the state legislature on June 22, 1821, which called for "Officers in – Blue hunting shirts trimmed with red, white pantaloons and vest, black hat with a black cockade and red plume – noncoms to be uniformed as above, except hunting shirts trimmed with white, [and] white plumes."

The slavery issue, and the Kansas/Missouri Border War of 1856, had already sharply divided the state; but when Governor Claiborne F. Jackson, a strong Southern sympathizer, was inaugurated in 1861, he made it clear that he intended to stand by the South in the approaching conflict. The military companies which avowed the same cause tended to be of older American or Irish stock and filled the ranks of the 1st Missouri Brigade, Volunteer Militia, based at St Louis. Generally these companies were distinctively garbed, but a regimental uniform had been adopted by 1860. Commanded by Col A.R. Easton (who had led the "St Louis Legion" during the Mexican War), the 1st Missouri Volunteer Militia wore a uniform based on State Regulations of 1857, which in turn were based on various US Army regulations. Nine-button dark blue frock coats

GLOSSARY
of organizational terms

Beat or common militia Formed as a result of the Federal Militia Act of May 8, 1792. Each state in the Union was required to enrol its white male population between the ages of 18 and 45 into a militia of "Heavy Infantry."

Volunteer militia Specialized in artillery, cavalry, dragoons, light infantry or riflemen, and were fully uniformed and armed at their own expense, except when called into state service, when the state supplied arms. As such, they were exempt from beat militia requirements.

Kentucky State Guard Established by a militia law passed on March 5, 1860, which placed all male Kentuckians into one of three militia classifications – volunteer (or State Guard), enrolled, or reserve. The former enlisted for a period of five years.

Six-month Volunteers Organized on March 6, 1861, when the CS Congress authorized President Jefferson Davis to call out an unspecified number of state militia for six months' service. Later, on June 6, 1863, 49,500 men were called out for six-month service "within the state."

Twelve-month Volunteers 100,000 men were called out by the Confederate government for one year on March 6, 1861; a further 19,500 were raised on April 8, 1861; and 32,000 on April 16, 1861.

Twelve-month garrison duty On March 9, 1861, 7,700 volunteers were called out for one year to garrison Southern forts.

Maryland Line Militia Established on April 20, 1861 for the defence of Baltimore. Disbanded by the time Federal forces occupied the city on May 13 that year.

Missouri State Guard Organized May 10–June 13, 1861; called for 50,000 men from 18–45 years old, but received only about 7,000. Began to disband on December 2, 1861, but continued to serve as militia until September 1862.

Volunteers "for the war" On February 2, 1862, 500,000 men were called out by the Confederate government for three years or "for the war."

Conscripts On April 16, 1862, the President was authorized to draft all white males between 18 and 35 (with substitutes permitted), and the terms of all men already in service were extended to three years.

Maryland Line Established on June 22, 1863, and composed of the 2nd Infantry (aka 1st Battalion); 1st Cavalry Battalion; and 1st through 4th Artillery batteries. The 2nd Cavalry (Gilmor's) resisted joining the Maryland Line, preferring to act as partisan rangers.

Reserves 30,000 volunteers had been called out as a "reserve army corps" as needed on June 30, 1861. On February 17, 1864, the CS Congress authorized the establishment of reserve forces for state defence; these units were organized on various occasions thereafter.

of 1851 pattern were trimmed around the collar and cuffs with narrow cord in either sky-blue or white. Sky-blue trousers had broad white seam stripes, as prescribed for US infantry in 1847. Dress caps were of the 1851 "National Guard" pattern, with "eagle" plate and brass wreath with company letter inset, surmounted by a white wool pompon.

On July 7, 1857, the Pioneer Corps attached to this regiment were reported in the Louisville *Daily Courier*, of Kentucky, to be wearing a "Red coat and sash, white pants," and carrying "a black hachet [sic]," when they paraded at that city on the Fourth of July. By 1861 this corps wore blue frock coats, trimmed with red and gold lace; dark gray pants with wide red seam stripes; bearskin caps with red bag, cord and tassels, plus red, white and blue plume; and high black leather boots. They were also required to wear full beards. When they paraded in celebration of the 129th anniversary of the birthday of George Washington on February 22, 1861, the St Louis National Guard, also known as the Engineer Corps of National Guards, under Maj G.M. Pritchard, wore blue frock coats edged with yellow lace, with pattern 1851 gilt engineer castle insignia on collar and dress cap.

The individual companies of the 1st Missouri reserved distinctive uniforms for special occasions. Commanded by Capt Martin Burke, the St Louis Grays (Co A) wore light gray tail coats with sky-blue facings and epaulettes, black dress caps, and light gray pants with wide blue seam stripes. A predominantly Irish unit, the Emmet Guards (Co D) wore blue tail coats faced with buff, and sky-blue pants with buff seam stripes. Also mostly Irish, the Washington Blues (Co E) were formed in 1857 as an offshoot of the Washington Guards of the same city. Commanded by a former British soldier, Capt Joseph M. Kelly, this unit wore dark blue frock coats with light blue facings and sky-blue pants. Their accoutrements included whitened buff leather waist belts and white webbing cartridge box slings. Both of these companies adopted bearskin caps and, according to the *Daily Missouri Democrat*, the latter paraded on January 8, 1861, in celebration of the 46th anniversary of the Battle of New Orleans wearing their "shakoes or Grenadier caps."

In preparation for going into camp at the end of April 1861, the Washington Blues were ordered to assemble at their Armory wearing "the Regimental uniform – with fatigue cap and black belt," plus knapsacks. On the same occasion Capt Charles L. Rogers, commanding the Sarsfield Guard, ordered his company to appear in "Uniform, regimental complete; knapsacks with overcoat inside and blankets strapped on flat, [with] canteens and haversacks." When the pro-Southern militia gathered in Camp Jackson at Lindell's Grove on May 3, 1861, the Engineer Corps were ordered to wear "blue jacket, grey pants, and engineer cap." The remainder of the 1st Missouri wore fatigue uniforms of US regulation pattern, plus forage caps.

A Missouri militiaman from Jefferson City, tentatively identified as Richard A. Basye, wearing full dress. The 1851 pattern cap displays an 1821 cockade eagle in lieu of the usual pompon eagle, above a militia-style wreath. Normally the latter had letters or numerals inset, and their absence here suggests either lack of availability, or that his unit was newly organized and not fully uniformed. His dark blue frock coat and sky-blue pants are probably trimmed white, in line with earlier US Army 1847 regulations for infantry. The worsted epaulettes and the pompon on his cap would also have been white. If possible, his oval "US" belt plate would have been changed for one bearing "MVM" or the state seal once the Civil War began. (Courtesy Myron W. Gwimmer)

Published in St Louis during 1854, this detail from the sheet music cover for the "St Louis National Guard March" shows the two types of full dress worn by that unit. The man at left wears a dark blue cap and a matching coat with shorter skirts than customary for the period, with sky-blue trousers. Although there was a Pioneer section of the National Guard, the man at right wears a scarlet tailcoat and bearskin reminiscent of a grenadier. (Lester S. Levy Collection of Sheet Music, Special Collections, Sheridan Libraries, The Johns Hopkins University)

Becoming alarmed at the growing presence of Unionist "Wide Awakes," or Lincoln supporters, among the German community in their city, prosecessionists met at Washington Hall on January 7–8, 1861, and recruited the "Minute Men of Missouri." The headquarters of the Southern Rights Democrats at the Berthold Mansion on 5th and Pine streets became their main recruiting station. By the beginning of March the Minute Men were described in the city press as being "armed with muskets" but "very unmilitary." Initially organized into a battalion of five companies by Gen Daniel Frost, they were mustered into the Missouri State Guard on February 13, 1861.

Influenced by the zouave military fashion, especially after the visit to that city on August 10, 1860, of the celebrated United States Zouave Cadets of Illinois commanded by Elmer Ellsworth, some companies of the 2nd Missouri adopted a dark gray zouave jacket and full pants, trimmed with black cord, gray shirt, and gray cap with black top. Officers wore dark gray frock coats with black collar and cuffs. At least one company of the 1st Regiment, the St Louis Artillery, may also have worn a similar zouave-style uniform.

On May 3, 1861 the 1st and 2nd Missouri gathered at Camp Jackson outside St Louis intent on taking over the US Arsenal in the city. Captured by pro-Unionist forces under Capt Nathaniel Lyon seven days later, they were subsequently demobilized; but many of them made their way to Memphis, Tennessee, where they formed the 1st Missouri Volunteer Infantry (Bowen's). They fought for the Confederacy at Shiloh, Corinth, and Hatchie Bridge, being captured at Vicksburg on July 4, 1863.

Missouri State Guard

In response to the Federal capture of the pro-Confederate militia at Camp Jackson in May, 1861, the Missouri state government at Jefferson City passed the Military Act four days later; this empowered the governor to "suppress rebellion and repel invasion," since the Federal government was viewed as hostile by the State Legislature. This measure included the formation of the Missouri State Guard, whose "active force of the line" was to be enlisted for a period of seven years in peace time, with Governor Jackson as its commander-in-chief and former Governor Sterling Price in command of all field forces. Composed of men aged from 18 to 45, the Missouri State Guard was drawn from the existing militia, supplemented by the enlistment of newly formed volunteer companies; volunteers were preferred, but local division commanders could draft individuals as needed. At its peak the State Guard amounted to about 7,000 men formed into some 62 poorly organized battalions, divided into nine military divisions of the state, each division representing a congressional district. Although these units began to disband on December 2, 1861, they continued to serve as militia until September 1862.

A board was established under the provisions of the Military Act to prescribe a uniform for the new state army. While uniformed volunteer militia companies were not required to adopt the uniform when mustered into the Guard, the law provided that the state uniform was to become mandatory when those companies found it necessary to renew their existing clothing. However, as this force saw combat slightly over a month after the passage of the bill, a state uniform was never adopted, and many of the enlistees joined the ranks either in the uniform of their company or in civilian dress. Indeed, of his arrival at Gen Price's encampment at Booneville in May 1861, Ephraim McD. Anderson, who enlisted in Co G, 2nd Infantry Regt, recalled: "Instead of seeing troops, as most of us anticipated, finely equipped and handsomely uniformed, we found the men with arms similar to our own ... and their clothes, generally in rags; the supply taken from home was exhausted or worn out, and they had not been able to replenish it."

Commanded by MajGen Sterling Price, the Missouri State Guard was forced to retire to the southwestern corner of the state, where they repelled the Federal columns sent to destroy them. Captain Otto C. Lademann, of the Federal 3rd Missouri Infantry, recalled of the battle of Carthage, July 5 1861, that "The enemy had no uniforms being entirely clad in homespun butternut jeans worn by every Missouri farmer in those days." The acting Adjutant General of the State Guard, Col Thomas L. Snead, observed of his comrades that "In all their motley array there was hardly a uniform to be seen, and then, and throughout all the brilliant campaign on which they were about to enter, there was nothing to distinguish their officers, even a general, from the men in the ranks, save a bit of red flannel, or a piece of cotton cloth, fastened to the shoulder, or to the arm, of the former."

One of those arriving at the Confederate recruiting camp at Cowskin Prairie, in southwest Missouri, was Peter D. Lane, a member of Capt D.C. Stone's company of Henry County volunteers (afterwards a private in the 16th Missouri Infantry). Lane recalled: "We had not been long encamped here until it was found necessary to appoint a number of Provost Guards whose business it was to travel about through camp and the surrounding country in order to arrest all soldiers

The St Louis Grays, 1st Missouri Volunteer Militia, are depicted in this lithograph from a sheet music cover wearing summer full dress: gray tail coats trimmed with sky-blue, and black dress caps with light-colored pompons. The musicians leading the parade, uniformed in darker frock coats with plastron fronts and 1851 caps, may or may not be attached to this unit. (Lester S. Levy Collection of Sheet Music, Special Collections, Sheridan Libraries, The Johns Hopkins University)

ABOVE **This *carte de visite* copy of an earlier ambrotype surfaced at Springfield, MO, and shows a member of an unknown volunteer militia infantry unit. He wears a single-breasted tailcoat with three rows of nine buttons, blind buttonhole trim on the faced collar, and five buttons on the faced cuff flaps. He has a small heart-shaped device pinned below his top central button, and a scabbarded socket bayonet is just visible on his waist belt. (Author's collection)**

ABOVE RIGHT **According to a period label glued to its reverse side, this unidentified tintype of a Confederate of possibly mixed racial origins was photographed at the studio of "R.F. Adams, Kirkwood, Mo." A community with strong Confederate affiliations, Kirkwood lay about 50 miles west of St Louis in Missouri. His thick gray woollen outer garment is either an overcoat or frock coat with collar turned down, or an overcoat without a cape. Underneath this he wears a gray shell jacket fastened with small brass military buttons. (Author's collection)**

found committing depredations of any kind and also to prevent the firing of guns in or near camp, & other officers were to have camp kept clean and nice. These guards wore a red riband around their shoulders as a token of their office and a passport for them at any time, for they were not to be halted by our guards."

However, sufficient evidence exists to indicate that uniforms were worn by some units within the Missouri State Guard. In May 1861, the Glasgow *Weekly Times*, of Howard County, noted the "handsome appearance" of the Glasgow Guards in their "semi-uniforms." The company, raised in Monroe County by Capt R.E. Dunn, presented a "fine, soldierly appearance" in its uniforms. The Monticello Grays, a cavalry unit in the Second Division, was the only uniformed company in its battalion, while a Scotland County company was "handsomely uniformed" when it prepared for war. In Benton and Jackson counties uniforms of the appropriate color were sewn for the Warsaw Blues, Warsaw Grays, and Independence Grays. Of two Saline County companies organized before hostilities began, the Saline Mounted Rifles were "neatly uniformed in gray," while the Saline Jackson Guards reported to Jefferson City in May "well uniformed and drilled," attracting the attention of all who saw them.

In his book *With Porter in North Missouri*, Joseph A. Mudd of the Jackson Guards mentions a brief contact with the Callaway Guards as he marched to join forces with Gen Sterling Price. "About three miles from Fayette, Howard County, we came up with a strong company from Fulton, commanded by Captain D.H. McIntyre clad in gray uniforms and armed with Enfield rifles." Ephraim Anderson had a similar experience when he observed a company from Paris in Monroe County; he recalled them as "a fine body of men, handsomely uniformed, and with a look decidedly military." During the siege of Lexington in September 1861, Anderson's attention was attracted to the 3rd Missouri Infantry, commanded by

Col Theodore Brace, and containing a number of companies that made a "showy and military appearance" in their varied uniforms.

Raised in Polk County, the Bolivar Company wore brown jeans with a red calico stripe an inch wide on the outer seam. A veteran reported in the Columbia *Herald* in September 1903 that the Columbia Grays wore "Gray St Charles coats with dark blue trim and gray trousers." The DeKalb Guards acquired black pants with yellow seam stripes to indicate their cavalry service, plus gray hunting shirts and caps. The LaGrange Guards adopted gray caps and shirts with blue trimmings, white pants with blue stripes and black belts. Made up mostly of Irishmen from St Louis, the 1st Missouri Light Artillery, commanded by Capt Henry Guibor, originally wore hats with red bands and rosettes, the brim turned up at one side with a button, and white jean suits. Several units designating themselves as "Rangers" appear to have worn quite colorful uniforms. The Plattin Rangers wore red caps and shirts with gray trousers, while the Polk County Rangers sported red zouave pantaloons with their gray jackets.

With the approach of the first winter of the war some Missouri troops had to depend on help from other states for clothing. On October 5, 1861, the Natchez *Daily Courier*, of Mississippi, reported that the "Confederate Sewing Society" at that city had been "actively engaged in making up garments for the Missouri volunteers." By this time the Missouri State Guard was dwindling in numbers as men fell ill or deserted. Those that remained in the ranks were informed by Governor Jackson at Greenfield, in Dade County, that "a large supply of clothing, boots and shoes had been purchased, and would be forwarded with as little delay as possible." According to Ephraim Anderson, this was "welcome tidings to most of the men, many being already bare-footed." Very limited supplies were issued the next month while the army was encamped near Neosho, but nothing like "a sufficiency, as many who were actually suffering got none," recalled Anderson:

Three pair of shoes were issued to our company, its proportion of what came to the division: there were eleven men in the company who needed them very badly, myself among the number; all of us had something in the way of boots or shoes, but in a very sorry condition, and so difficult was it to ascertain whose feet were nearest upon the ground, that we were ordered to stand up in a row for inspection. We all walked out and formed, each hoping to be one of the lucky fellows; looking down the line to see what sort of a chance mine was, I discovered several pair of bare feet, the owners of which had been smart enough to leave their shoes or boots behind; though my prospect now was anything but flattering, I still held my place until all were ordered to break ranks except the barefooted part of the squad; there were five, who drew straws for the prizes, the toes of the longest straws being left out in the fros or compelled to fall back on their reserves in the tents.

With the help of "strong and earnest persuasion," backed by "a gold piece," Anderson eventually acquired footwear in Neosho.

Emmitt MacDonald was captain of the St Louis Artillery, a company of the 1st Regt, Missouri Volunteer Militia, at the beginning of the Civil War. He went on to command the 3rd Battery, Missouri Light Artillery, CSA, and fought at Wilson's Creek, Lexington, and Pea Ridge. He wears a well-lined zouave-style gray jacket with a faced and trimmed collar, and trim on the cuff flaps and front edges. Just visible below the bottom of the collar at the front is a small, light-colored cord trefoil. His gray 1851 dress cap, with a lighter-colored band, has the cardboard stiffening removed to give the appearance of fatigue wear. A broad-bladed Bowie knife is partially concealed under his jacket. (Courtesy Wilson's Creek National Battlefield)

Volunteers and guerrillas

During the winter of 1861–62 many members of the Missouri State Guard were reorganized as volunteers into Confederate service, forming the First and Second Missouri brigades. Enlisting as a member of Co G, 2nd Missouri Infantry (Burbridge's), which was the first Confederate regiment organized in Missouri, Ephraim Anderson recorded the manner in which his unit were clothed at Boston Mountain, Arkansas, towards the end of February, 1862:

> Our regiment was uniformed here; the cloth was of rough and coarse texture, and the cutting and style would have produced a sensation in fashionable circles: the stuff was white, never having been colored, with the exception of a small quantity of dirt and a goodly supply of grease – the wool had not been purified by any application of water since it was taken from the back of the sheep. In pulling off and putting on the clothes, the olfactories were constantly exercised with a strong odor of that animal. Our brigade was the only body of troops that had these uniforms issued to them, and we were often greeted with a chorus of ba-a-a's... Our clothes, however, were strong and serviceable, if we did look and feel somewhat sheepish in them.

Some elements of the State Guard joined guerrilla bands which continued to operate in Missouri. The most notable of these was that led by William Clarke Quantrill, who, in time, developed "a dress peculiar to themselves which became known up and down the border. Its distinguishing item was a 'guerrilla shirt.'" Patterned after "the hunting coat of the Western plainsmen," this shirt was "cut low in front, the slit narrowing to a point above the belt and ending in a rosette [sic]. The garment had four big pockets, two in the breast, and ranged in color from brilliant red to homespun butternut. They were made by the mothers, wives, and sweethearts of the guerrillas, and many were elaborately decorated with colored needlework."

Some Missouri volunteers and guerrillas fought in captured blue Federal uniforms. When elements of the State Guard captured a militia arsenal at Memphis in Scotland County, Joseph Mudd recorded that "We also secured a number of Federal uniforms. A blouse fell to me, which I wore only for comfort." The fact that Missourians, plus Confederate volunteers in other states, wore blue for whatever reason eventually prompted General Orders No.100 from the US Adjutant General's office, dated April 24, 1863, which stipulated that "Troops who fight in the uniform of their enemies, without any plain, striking and uniform mark of distinction of their own, can expect no quarter."

Henderson Duval of the Missouri State Guard wears a plain civilian shirt tucked into military trousers with light, possibly gold-colored seam stripes. He appears to be holding a Tucker and Sherrod .44cal revolver, while a single-shot horse pistol is pushed into the waistband of his pants. (Courtesy Wilson's Creek National Battlefield)

Military suppliers

Due to their withdrawal to the southwestern corner of the state in June 1861, the Missouri volunteers and State Guard units had great difficulty in obtaining uniforms, arms, and equipage. Likely local suppliers of clothing to pro-Confederate forces before they withdrew from St Louis included Woolf's Shirt Depot, on North Third and North Fourth streets, who advertised "grey flannel over shirts for sale cheap" in the *Daily Missouri Democrat* on May 2, 1861. In the same city, C.B. Hubbell Jr & Co stocked "Several thousand yards of Heavy Grey Flannels suitable for military purposes." A notice from Gill & Brothers, at 95 North Main Street, appeared in columns of the *Tri-Weekly Missouri Republican* of May 9, 1861, selling "Military Outfits" including "gray, blue and red flannel – hickory, check and calico overshirts. White and gray wool undershirts and drawers. India rubber coats and blankets. Berlin and buck gloves. White and drab gauntlets." On June 15 military buttons and trimmings were available at "the lowest rates" in the same journal via Staddler, Brothers & Company. Headgear was for sale at Keevil's "Great National Hat Hall" on Broadway in St Louis. Footwear could be had at Dickson, Orr & Co, who advertised "1,000 Cases – boots and shoes bought at panic prices." Bell, Tilden & Co offered "Army Blankets – one thousand pairs blue blankets. One thousand pairs grey blankets. Two hundred pairs white mackinaw blankets."

Entries found in an account book for the Missouri State Guard indicate that, as the pro-Confederate forces withdrew into the southwest corner of the state in mid-1861, their Quartermaster purchased clothing and bolts of cloth from various suppliers. Most goods were acquired from Fayetteville, in Johnson County, on July 16. J.W. Walker provided "108 pr Brogans" and "21 hats"; W.J. Stewart supplied "30 yds canton flannel... 33 assorted hats... 8 prs lined Buck gloves... 6 pea coats" and "15 Fancy shirts," among other goods. Meanwhile F. Ruff, at Ozark in Christian County, sold "27 yds plain lindsay... 26½ yds red flannel... 26 yds yellow flannel." One of the most unusual purchases was made on July 3, when Hyatt & Allen, of Lamar in Bartow County, provided "24 Buffalo robes," which presumably indicates preparation for a winter campaign.

In the matter of martial music, drums, fifes and "cavalry horns," plus "any other Musical Instrument used for Military Purposes," could be obtained at "The Great Drum Depot" run by John L. Peters & Brother on North Fifth Street in St Louis, according to the *Daily Missouri Demoncrat* of May 1, 1861.

Insignia

A number of distinctive insignia and devices were worn by the volunteer militia of Missouri up to the outbreak of the Civil War. According to Hyde and Conrad's history of St Louis, members of the 2nd Missouri wore a "large polished brass clasp, with 'M.V.M.' in raised letters." Further examples worn by individual companies of the 1st Missouri are recorded in the same source. Reflecting their ethnic origins, the Emmet Guards carried on their shoulder belt plate "a silver wreath of shamrock enclosing the initial letters, 'E.G.'" The shoulder belt plate of the National Guards bore the "silver monogram of the

Photographed at his home town of Springfield, MO, on October 12, 1861, Daniel Dorsey Berry Jr enlisted in a company of the Missouri State Guard commanded by Leonidas C."Dick" Campbell. He wears a distinctive shirt with trim on the collar, cuffs, buttoned front and pocket tops. The brim of his hat is pinned up with a metal button and is embellished with a black ostrich feather, and he holds a straight-bladed militia officer's sword. (J. Dale West Collection)

company – 'N.G.' – in the center." As further evidence of the Irish influence in St Louis, the Washington Guards bore a "gilt spread-eagle" on the front of their dress caps "beneath a gilt harp entwined with shamrocks." The shoulder belt plate of the Washington Blues consisted of a brass plate with "a bronze bust of [George] Washington ... entwined with a silver wreath of shamrocks."

The Military Act of May 14, 1861, stated that: "The coat of arms of Missouri shall be worn on the buttons of all uniforms of the Missouri State Guard." Buttons bearing the Missouri state seal adopted in 1822, and showing two grizzly bears supporting a central shield with a helmet serving as a crest, were produced in the North during antebellum times by the Scovill Manufacturing Company of Waterbury, Connecticut, and Smith & Young Company of New York.

Arms and equipage

Due to the circumstances in which they were raised, Missouri troops serving the Confederacy carried a great variety of arms. Originally a member of the Ashland Guards, of Boone County, Andrew McLean McGregor fought under Col John S. Marmaduke at Booneville on June 17, 1861, after which he recorded that his unit had "no ammunition, shotguns and squirrel rifles were our arms." Having enlisted in Capt Jack Stone's company, of Lexington County, by the following July his unit had "a lot of old flint lock guns. If one of them was ever fired I did not know it."

Of his original unit formed at Middle Grove in Monroe County, Ephraim Anderson recalled that "Our company had about eight guns, and these were the common rifle and double-barreled shot-gun. I had with me one of the latter." Enlisted shortly afterwards in a company of the 6th Infantry, Third Division, Missouri State Guard, he recorded that "We were [then] armed with shot guns and rifles and had among us a good many revolvers."

Enlisting in the Missouri State Guard at Paris, Monroe County, C.M. Farthing wrote that "mounted men and half grown boys poured in from the country, each carrying a double or single barrel shotgun, or a squirrel rifle. Some were armed with

Privates S.W. Stone, California Guards, and P.S. Alexander, Moniteau County Rangers, of the Missouri State Guard, portrayed at Jefferson City in May 1861 soon after the formation of the State Guard. The only sign of possible military dress in this image is the cap worn by Stone, who is armed with a musket, and wears a fancy tooled-leather holster and double-buckle belt which also supports a Bowie knife. Alexander holds a double-barreled shotgun, and has a wide leather shoulder belt which probably supports a cartridge box. A large Bowie knife is stuck in his belt, and a bouquet of wild flowers adorns his hat. (Courtesy Wilson's Creek National Battlefield)

corn [sic] or hand-made knives, fastened by leather straps about their waists or to their saddle horns, and one carried a real sword, an heirloom of the Revolution." Given the lack of equipment, men with experience in leatherwork were much valued; Frank L. Pitts of Co G, 2nd Missouri Infantry was detailed home to "manufacture in the shop of himself and brother, T.W. Pitts, a quantity of belts, straps and sheaths for the big knives and revolvers the command was armed with."

Some State Guard companies were issued weapons seized at the US arsenal at Liberty, Clay County, on April 21, 1861. These probably consisted of about 1,500 pieces, including unaltered flintlock muskets and caliber .69 converted muskets. A further 500 flintlock muskets were requisitioned from the State of Virginia by the CS Ordnance department. Issued to the 2nd Infantry and 3rd Infantry Battalion, 1st Division, Missouri State Guard, about 600 of the above muskets had been altered to percussion at the Memphis Arsenal by February 1862. Included in a report entitled "Encampment of the State Regiments" published in the *Daily Missouri Democrat* on May 7, 1861, 50 men in the 2nd Infantry, State Guard were described as still having "no guns."

Organized for Confederate service on June 22, 1861, the 1st Missouri Infantry (Bowen's) received 545 muskets, plus one box of bayonets, from the Ordnance Bureau at Richmond, Virginia, towards the end of August of that year. Reorganized for Confederate service by the beginning of 1862, the 4th, 5th and 6th Missouri Infantry probably received "old rifles" converted into "Mississippi rifles with a saber bayonet"; while many of the 1st, 2nd, and 3rd Missouri Cavalry were issued "single barrel shotguns ... converted into carbines." In winter quarters at Springfield during the same period, Ephraim Anderson recalled that "While here our shot-guns were turned over to the Ordnance department, and those who did not have muskets were furnished with them."

In the case of local supply, firearms were for sale in St Louis from Horace E. Dimmock, who stated confidently in the *Tri-Weekly Missouri Republican* on May 16, 1861, that the country would be "safe so long as the majority of western hunters, trappers and sporting patriots" bought his "Guns, Rifles, Pistols and Ammunition." He further offered to provide "Military Companies and State Governments with all kinds of fixed ammunition for military arms; expanding ball cartridges for rifled muskets, breech-loading guns and pistols." In the same city, Savory & Mallory sold "Colts 4 inch revolver (Pocket)," plus M1851 "Navy size" Colt revolvers.

At Liberty in Clay County, Moses Dickson, proprietor of the City Gunsmith Shop, announced that he had on hand and was "constantly manufacturing ... Rifles and Shot Guns." He also advertised "a fine stock of Colt's, Sharp's and Allen's Pistols, Bowie Knives, Shot Bags, Powder and Pistol Flasks."

Equipage was also issued to volunteers for Confederate service at Springfield. According to Ephraim Anderson, his unit "drew new accoutrements, which had just been brought up – cartridge-boxes and belts with 'C.S.' upon them. Many of the men, however, retained their old United States ones, considering them better than those we were drawing." They were also issued knapsacks and blankets. Some of the latter were of "very superior quality, and many made of fine pieces of carpet were among them."

KENTUCKY

Antebellum militia

With opinion divided over the issue of slavery and State's Rights on the eve of the Civil War, it became apparent to military experts in Kentucky that the militia system of that state was in need of total reform. The enrolled militia had been invalidated by a new state constitution in 1850, but revived the following year because the state was not yet prepared to depend on the volunteer militia system. The Annual Abstract of Returns of the Militia of the US for 1857 listed a total of 88,858 militiamen in Kentucky, of whom 86,000 were enrolled militia. The remainder – consisting of 900 cavalry, 1,000 artillery, and 700 riflemen – were uniformed volunteer militia, organized into several regiments and battalions by 1860. Originally formed on January 21, 1839, the 1st Kentucky Infantry, or Louisville Legion, was redesignated the Louisville Battalion, under Maj Thomas H. Hunt, on May 7 of that year. About the same time, the Lexington Battalion was formed from the old 2nd Kentucky Infantry, and combined with the Kentucky River Battalion during November 1860.

As with all other states, the volunteer militia of Kentucky wore a wide variety of colorful uniforms with flying plumes. Attending a drill competition at the Gallatin Fair in August 1860, the Marion Rifles of Louisville had a full dress "a la French Zouave" consisting of "a light cap of red and grey; tunics of grey and red, trimmed with blue velvet and gold lace; loose trousers of red cloth, reaching to the calf of the leg; and gaiters of grey cloth, buttoned close about the ankles." Their fatigue dress had been reported earlier, in the Louisville *Daily Courier* of February 23, 1858, as consisting of "a military cap, dark jacket and pants, striped with green velvet, edged with gold; their arms – as the name imports – that famous weapon, the Western rifle." In 1860 this was further described as "a brown frock coat with a double row of army buttons in front; pants of the same material with velvet stripe down the sides, caps of the same cloth, with the initials 'M.R.' in gilt, on the front."

Following their organization by future Confederate Gen Simon Bolivar Buckner in 1857, the Citizen Guards paraded for the anniversary of the birthday of George Washington, on February 22, 1858, on which occasion the *Courier* commented that they wore "an exceedingly tasty dress" consisting of "Gray cap and coat, and pants striped with gold lace." By 1860 this unit had also adopted tall bearskins and gray frock coats as part of their full dress of gray trimmed with black and gold. In May 1861, the Citizen Guards entered the ranks of the 2nd Regiment, Kentucky State Guard,

commanded by Col Thomas H. Hunt. Also from Louisville, the Falls City Guard wore "a blue military hat, topped with falling plume of white and yellow, and blue cloth coat and pants, with military stripe." The Madison Guards adopted "Gray pants, blue coat, infantry hat" during 1857. When raised in Lexington by future Confederate raider John Hunt Morgan during the same year, the Lexington Rifles adopted rifle-green caps and frock coats. Of the same city, the Lexington Chasseurs paraded on the Fourth of July, 1860, under the command of Capt Sanders D. Bruce wearing blue frock coats, scarlet pants with gold lace seam stripes, and the "modern military hat with white and red plume," or 1854 pattern dress cap.

The Union Grays, of Georgetown, wore gray tailcoats with three rows of buttons, white webbing belts, gray pants with wide black seam stripes, and 1851 dress caps with black bands and fountain plumes. The Bedford Rifles, of Trimble County, wore "blue pants, with yellow stripe, navy blue frock coats, cadet pattern; blue cloth caps with red plush plumes." Despite their name, the Flat Rock Grays of Bourbon County marched off to war in what Lt Lot D. Young called "'clawhammer' blue broadcloth and gold buttons," which indicates that blue tailcoats formed part of their full dress uniform. This unit became Co H, 4th Kentucky Infantry in 1861.

Judging from the surviving uniform of Lineas Richmond, the Oak Grove Rangers, organized at Hopkinsville in Christian County by Thomas G. Woodward, wore a cadet-gray tailcoat with two rows of seven brass eagle "C" buttons connected by bars of wide red braid, solid red collar and

Published by D.P. Faulds & Co in 1858, this sheet music cover for the "Louisville Citizen Guards March/Quickstep" shows an officer and first sergeant wearing the full dress uniform of the Citizen Guards. This unit enlisted into Confederate service as Co B, 9th Kentucky Infantry (Caldwell's), and fought with the "Orphan Brigade" at Murfreesboro, Chickamauga, Atlanta, and during the campaign in the Carolinas. (Lester S. Levy Collection of Sheet Music, Special Collections, Sheridan Libraries, The Johns Hopkins University)

matching cuffs trimmed with elaborate trefoils. Trousers of the same color had broad red seam stripes with the lower legs sheathed in leather fastened by five brass buttons, to protect from wear against saddle skirting and stirrup straps. Members of this unit enlisted in Confederate service as Cos A and B, 1st Kentucky Cavalry, near Camp Boone in Montgomery County, Tennessee, on June 25, 1861. In conjunction with possible red trim worn on later clothing, their commander had them lay a stovepipe upon a wagon axle and ordered them to pose as artillery during the attack on Federal forces at Clarksburg, Tennessee, in 1862. The Union garrison, knowing that it could not hold out against artillery, surrendered forthwith.

Photographed at Camp Boone, KY, during August 1860, the Jefferson Rifles are seen at rest after parade. Many still wear their dark green frock coats and dress caps, while others have changed into their gray, pleated hunting shirts. (Margaret I. King Library, University of Kentucky)

Kentucky State Guard

A graduate of the class of 1844 at the US Military Academy, and for several years Instructor of Military Tactics at that post, Mexican War veteran Simon Bolivar Buckner resigned from the US Army in 1855, but continued his military career as captain of the Citizen Guards of Louisville. Under instructions from pro-Southern Governor Beriah Magoffin, he drew up plans for an entirely new militia system for Kentucky which included the State Guard, a corps of uniformed volunteer militia created via act of legislature on March 5, 1860, to serve for a period of five years. By the end of August of that year the Kentucky State Guard consisted of five battalions, embodying a total of 49 infantry, artillery, and mounted companies, which included many of the antebellum volunteer militia companies.

By November 1860 enough State Guard companies had been organized in the Lexington area to form a regiment, and Col Roger W. Hanson was appointed commander of the 1st Infantry, Kentucky State Guard. The 2nd Infantry was organized in Louisville by April, 1861, with Thomas H. Hunt as executive officer; and during the following month the 3rd and 4th Regts were established, with Thomas L. Crittenden and Lloyd Tilghman in command. By the beginning of June 1861 the first three regiments of Kentucky State Guard had been organized into a brigade under the command of Thomas Crittenden. (He was the brother of Unionist Senator John Crittenden, author of the failed proposal to avert civil war by extending the Missouri Compromise line to the Pacific in 1860, who was eventually appointed brigadier-general in the Union army and was brevetted for gallantry at Stones River in 1863.)

Appointed commander-in-chief and Inspector General of this new force with the rank of major-general, Buckner revisited West Point to obtain ideas for the uniform to be worn by this new corps.

OPPOSITE **The officers of the eleven companies of Kentucky State Guard present at Camp Boone gather for a group photograph in August 1860. Headgear varies from bearskins and 1851 dress hats to tricorn hats, while the uniforms are of gray, blue or green cloth. (Margaret I. King Library, University of Kentucky)**

After several days of discussion with instructor of artillery Rufus Saxton, he decided upon a uniform of cadet-gray trimmed with black, silver and gold, which happened to be the main colors of the uniforms worn by both the West Point cadets and Buckner's own Citizens' Guard.

General Orders No.5, issued on July 18, 1860, defined the styles and colors of the uniform of the Kentucky State Guard: "The full-dress coat being a frock of 'cadet' gray cloth, trowsers same cloth, and patterned after those of the French infantry of the line. The epaulette was not to be worn, but in its place a shoulder strap was adopted, thus doing away with the square-shouldered appearance, caused by the epaulette, and allowing the symmetrical bend and form of the shoulder to be seen. The fatigue dress is exactly similar to that of the French Chasseurs à Pied."

By August 1860 Buckner and other officers of the Kentucky State Guard began to appear in the new full-dress uniform. Generals and field officers wore a double-breasted cadet-gray frock coat, with collar and cuffs faced with black velvet, based on 1857 US Army regulations. That worn by Buckner, which survives in the collection of the Museum of the Confederacy, displayed the collar rank insignia for a general officer – an embroidered silver shield flanked by two five-point stars. The unusual shoulder straps (see Plate E3) carried a silver spread eagle on black velvet edged with two rows of silver lace, edged with thin gold cord.

Other Kentuckian general officers photographed in this uniform include Sterling Price, George B. Crittenden, Humphrey Marshall, and Benjamin H. Helm (the latter being Abraham Lincoln's brother-in-law, who was eventually killed at Chickamauga). At some point in early 1861 the general officer's version of this uniform was misconstrued as the regulation dress of the new Confederacy, and convenient photographs were altered to show the distinctive collar and shoulder devices on prominent Southern generals such as Thomas J. "Stonewall" Jackson.

As a field officer with the rank of colonel, Assistant Quartermaster-General Frank Tryon wears a double-breasted frock coat with a silver embroidered "extended hand" either side of the collar, echoing the 1792 state coat of arms of Kentucky featuring two men shaking hands. His square-ended shoulder straps feature double lace edging and a silver embroidered leaf. (Margaret I. King Library, University of Kentucky)

Appointed to the Subsistence Department of the Kentucky State Guard with the rank of captain on September 1, 1860, Philip Vacaro wears a single-breasted frock coat with rank denoted by a silver embroidered eagle on the collar; his shoulder straps are plain apart from the edging. (Margaret I. King Library, University of Kentucky)

Photographs showing officers of lesser grades wearing this uniform indicate a complicated system of collar and shoulder strap rank insignia. Field-grade officers – such as Col Benjamin Helm, who served as Assistant Inspector-General, and Maj James A. Beattie, who was appointed Judge-Advocate – wore a double-breasted frock coat with a silver embroidered "extended hand" either side of the collar, echoing the 1792 state coat of arms of Kentucky featuring two men shaking hands. Shoulder straps featured a silver embroidered leaf. The coat worn by company-grade officers – such as Philip Vacaro, who was a captain in the Subsistence Department by 1861 – was single-breasted with black cloth collar, cuffs, and plain shoulder straps; rank was otherwise indicated by a silver embroidered "eagle" either side of the collar. Staff NCOs wore the same pattern coat with plain black collar and shoulder straps. Officers' caps of chasseur pattern were cadet-gray with a black band, quartered with gold lace trim. Trousers were also cadet-gray with light-colored, possibly gold seam stripes. Brown leather or canvas buttoned gaiters were worn by enlisted ranks.

The extent to which the full dress uniform was adopted by the rank and file of the Kentucky State Guard is unclear. Similarly, the French Chasseurs à Pied-style uniform appears not to have seen widespread use. According to Buckner's wife, a "Hunting shirt," in imitation of "the clothes of the pioneers of the state," was encouraged as a fatigue dress. That worn by Gen Buckner himself is held today in the collection of the Museum of the Confederacy. The Jefferson Rifles, a volunteer militia company organized by John Hunt Morgan, wore a similar style of shirt.

However, a report published in the *Kentucky Statesman* of Lexington on April 30, 1861, indicates that volunteer companies, at least in Fayette County, were "conforming very generously in the adoption of uniforms to the recommendation of the State Guard." The "old companies," it stated, were changing their "former handsome dress for a plain but serviceable

Staff officer and non-commissioned officers of the Kentucky State Guard at Camp Boone, near Louisville, Kentucky, wearing examples of the uniform prescribed for their corps on July 18, 1860. To the left of the top-hatted figure stands Col Frank Tryon, Assistant Quartermaster General and Assistant Commissary-General; at right are Quartermaster Staff Sergeant Philip Vacaro (later captain in the Subsistence Department) and Staff Sergeant C. Brockenborough. (Margaret I. King Library, University of Kentucky)

garb of Kentucky jeans." The *Statesman* further explained that lower production costs placed this uniform within the price range of the humblest of privates, and encouraged newly forming units to complete their organization. On September 17, 1861, the Louisville *Weekly Journal* reported seeing members of the Citizen Guards leave for Camp Boone via the Nashville Depot in that city "with their uniforms on," which is a probable reference to this plainer clothing.

Opposed to the prospect of enrollment for a period of five years' service in the Kentucky State Guard, some of those who wished to hold themselves in readiness to serve the pro-Southern state governor enlisted in the ranks of the "Minute Men of Kentucky." The first of this body was organized in Louisville under the command of a "Captain Johnston" in January 1861.

Volunteer forces 1861–63

With the outbreak of hostilities in April 1861, Kentucky adopted a neutral position, and by September the state legislature had authorized the Military Board to disarm the State Guard. By this time most Kentuckians with Southern sympathies had made their way to the newly formed Confederate States to offer their services. Originally commanding a local volunteer militia company called the Paducah City Guards, Col Lloyd Tilghman organized for Confederate service seven companies of Kentucky State Guard, numbering 650 men, at Paducah in April 1861. These companies later made up the bulk of the 3rd Kentucky Infantry (Holt's), being mustered into Confederate service at Camp Boone in Tennessee on July 5, 1861.

Fire-brand secessionist Blanton Duncan formed another volunteer battalion at Louisville during March and April 1861, which included the Duncan Guards, Cornwall Guards, Bustard Guards, and Davis Guards. Hastily uniformed and equipped, most of this unit were reported in the Nashville *Daily Gazette* to have worn hunting shirts based on the Buckner pattern. Merged with another battalion at Harpers Ferry, Virginia, commanded by Thomas Taylor, these men established the 1st Kentucky Infantry, a twelve-month regiment which fought at Dranesville under J.E.B. Stuart, after which it served in D.R. Jones' brigade, Army of Northern Virginia. Numerous other Kentuckians crossed over the border into Tennessee during June 1861, and this led to the organization of the 2nd and 3rd Kentucky Infantry regiments, plus other units, at Camps Boone, Burnett, and Breckenridge.

As fresh volunteers formed further regiments in southern Kentucky and northern Tennessee they were provided with plainer uniforms of various patterns. The clothing of some of the Kentuckians under Taylor in Virginia was wearing out by July 1861; on the 27th of that month the

Published in Lexington, the pro-Southern *Kentucky Statesman* advertised cloth for uniforms. (Above) Massachusetts-born Richard Loud advised both Southern and Northern factions in the city of the suitability of his "Cadet Grey Jeans." Brother of the future Confederate raider John Hunt Morgan, R.C. Morgan (below) assured prospective customers of the "superior article of Jeans" produced at his factory. (Author's collection)

19

Louisville *Courier* reported that the Harrison Rifles – Co C, 1st Kentucky, commanded by Capt Joseph Desha – were in receipt of "a beautiful new uniform of grey cloth, the goods for which was manufactured ... by William Job & Co, a firm composed of gentlemen of the highest probity and most strict integrity, who have already a good degree of custom in Kentucky."

From September 1861 to the capture of Fort Donelson in February 1862 the southwestern part of Kentucky was occupied by Confederate forces. Wishing to see their state represented within the Confederacy, the Kentuckians in this force organized a "sovereignty convention," and in November 1861 passed an ordinance of secession, elected a state legislature, and ordered commissioners to the Southern Congress. As a result, Kentucky was admitted to the Confederate States on December 9, 1861.

By October 1861, a clothing shortage became evident. At Bowling Green, Kentucky, Quartermaster V.K. Stevenson was unable to supply adequate uniforms to Col Thomas H. Hunt's 5th Kentucky Infantry, and advised that company captains should supply only those men in the most need. At Clarksville, near Camp Boone, 200 women were put to work making clothing for the 2nd, 3rd, and 4th Kentucky Infantry regiments. Meanwhile, at Camp Alcorn near Hopkinsville, Kentucky, the Quartermaster admitted that he was "entirely deficient" of clothing.

Nonetheless, the fact that they were spared heavy campaigning service, and the large amount of clothing that volunteers brought with them, probably enabled Kentuckians to stay well uniformed until toward the end of 1861. In his recollections of service as an officer in the 4th Kentucky Cavalry, George D. Musgrove remarked that as a rule he was "fond of gay attire, his style being regulation cavalry boots, a red sash, a large black felt hat, of the slouch variety, with the brim of one side turned up and pinned to the side of the crown with a silver crescent or star, the whole surmounted by a huge, black ostrich plume."

As the 2nd Kentucky Cavalry, commanded by John Hunt Morgan, set out from Knoxville on its first raid in 1862, they were described as lacking "general uniforms," although some were in "new regulation gray, others in butternut jeans." Members of Cos E and F of this regiment were photographed wearing light gray seven- and eight-button shell jackets with solid (possibly yellow) facings on collar and cuffs; the cuffs appear to have been fastened by a row of six small buttons along the back seam. Marcellus J. Clarke

OPPOSITE **Samuel O. "One-Arm" Berry, Co A, 2nd Kentucky Cavalry, poses for the camera with Marcellus Jerome Clarke, alias "Sue Mundy." On March 15, 1865, three weeks before the end of the Civil War, 21-year-old Clarke was hanged as a Confederate guerrilla in Louisville, KY, as a crowd of thousands looked on; by the time of his execution he had earned a reputation as the region's most dangerous and enigmatic *female* outlaw. He wears a distinctive frock coat with facing color on collar and cuffs. The collar is also fastened at the neck by a small tab, while the cuffs have eight small "zouave-style" buttons on the tongue of facing extended over the back seam. (John Sickles Collection, USAMHI)**

OPPOSITE **William S. Sullivan, a private in Co H, 8th Kentucky Cavalry, wears what appears to be an early war ten- or 12-button shell jacket with trim (possibly yellow in color) around the collar and cuffs and down the front opening edge. (USAMHI)**

RIGHT **Organized in Madison County during August 1862, the 7th (later 11th) Kentucky Cavalry rode with John Hunt Morgan into Indiana and Ohio. Most of its personnel were captured at Buffington Island and New Lisbon, OH, in July 1863. Third Sgt Andrew M. McCord, Co B, wears the seven-button shell jacket with breast pocket worn by several Kentucky cavalry regiments, and holds a black felt 1858 pattern dress hat. He was captured at Buffington Island and imprisoned at Camp Douglas in Chicago, Illinois. (USAMHI)**

(alias "Sue Mundy") of Co B, 4th Kentucky Infantry (Trabue's), carried eight buttons on each of his cuffs; and 18 small buttons were sewn on the cuffs of a nine-button jacket worn by Thomas Bronston Collins, Co F, 11th Kentucky Cavalry (Chenault's). Most of these cavalrymen appear to have worn narrow-brimmed black felt hats; that worn by T.B. Collins was looped up on one side by a small five-point metal star.

Private Thomas W. Blandford, 8th Kentucky Infantry (Burnett's), wore a double-breasted mid-gray frock coat with two rows of seven Kentucky State buttons, an outside pocket set at an angle level on the left breast, a 1¼in high black collar and black pointed cuffs. It is held by the Museum of the Confederacy, and still has a small pin attached consisting of a dull silver star engraved with "KY," secured to which is a crescent engraved with "Nil Desperandum"; a red silk ribbon, probably the remains of a cockade, hangs from this pin. Members of both the 8th and 11th Kentucky Cavalry regiments were photographed wearing gray shell jackets with seven-button fronts and pockets let into the left breast. Some of these appear to have facing color (possibly yellow) on collar and cuffs.

In the winter of 1861/62 the 2nd Kentucky Infantry were furnished with hooded overcoats privately purchased for the regiment by Maj James W. Hewitt. That worn by David T.C. Weller, who served in Co C, survives in the Kentucky Military History Museum in Frankfort, Kentucky, and is believed to have been worn by him at Fort Donelson. The body and hood of this garment are of gray woollen jeans and appear to be undyed. Fastened by four widely spaced buttons, it is lined with blue-and-white striped twilled cotton ticking, and has a waist-height vertical pocket on the right side.

The 1st Kentucky Brigade (nicknamed the "Orphan Brigade" by Gen Breckenridge, after their sacrifice in life and limb at Murfreesboro in December 1862), was composed of the 2nd, 3rd, 4th, 6th, and 9th Kentucky Infantry. These regiments were in receipt of Confederate quartermaster-issue clothing, probably from the Columbus Depot, from late 1862 until the end of 1864.

Military suppliers

Described as one of the oldest and most reliable merchants in Louisville, John M. Armstrong advertised "State Guard suits" in the Louisville *Daily Journal* on May 11, 1861. Stating that they were prepared "to make up to order on the shortest notice for Companies of the state or Home Guards," Lieber, Griffin, Friedman & Co of the same city offered a variety of military items including "mixed blue and gray cloth, Kentucky state guard, eagle buttons and other trimmings." Owned by L. Richardson, the Louisville Woolen Mills produced "white and colored Jeans and Linsey." At Lexington,

Samuel Henry Payne, Co A, 8th Kentucky Cavalry, also wears a version of the seven-button cavalry shell jacket seen on several Kentuckians. In this case the collar is adorned either side with a small button, and it possibly has facing color trim on the collar and cuffs. (USAMHI)

ABOVE RIGHT Both privates in Co K, 8th Kentucky Cavalry, William H. Carter and William G. McCormick wear similar hats, jackets, trousers, and boots. Serving in Kentucky and during Morgan's raid through south-eastern Indiana and southern Ohio during July 1863, their regiment was not reorganized after its capture at Buffington Island. (USAMHI)

Massachusetts-born wool manufacturer Richard Loud advertised "Cadet Grey Jeans [suitable for] uniforms for the Kentucky State Guard," while local merchant tailor George A. Bowyer sewed the uniforms. Another factory in the same city owned by Richard C. Morgan, brother of John Hunt Morgan, reported in the *Kentucky Statesman* on April 30, 1861, that it had supplied several companies of State Guard with "a very superior article of jeans." At Glasgow, Barren County, during August 1861 ex-slave trader M.H. Maupin purchased 10,000 yards of Kentucky jeans from the Morgan factory, which he declared he would have "no difficulty in disposing of ... among his 'Southern Rights' friends."

Headgear was available at Louisville via Moses Levy, who advertised the "Military Cap Depot" on Market Street; while Alexander Craig produced "Military Caps" in the same city, and announced that officers' caps were "made to order." Military "Fatigue Caps" were to be had at Lexington from J.F. Thompson.

During the years preceding the Civil War the New York firm of James S. Smith & Sons produced tongue-and-wreath waist belt plates bearing the 1792 state coat of arms of Kentucky, which showed two men shaking hands above the motto "United We Stand, Divided We Fall." Buttons with the same device were made at Louisville by Wolf & Durringer, while several companies including Scovill Manufacturing Company, and Horstmann & Allien, of New York, produced the same in the Northern states. A shield-shaped plate for shoulder belts also bearing the Kentucky state arms was made by Horstmann in Philadelphia during April 1860. Situated at 223 Main Street, Louisville, David P. Faulds advertised "Drums and Fifes of every description" of his own manufacture in the *Daily Courier* on June 5, 1861.

Arms and equipage

In January 1861 the Adjutant-General of the Kentucky Militia reported that the state owned 11,283 muskets, 3,159 rifles, 2,873 sets of cavalry arms and accoutrements, plus 53 pieces of ordnance. By August of that year 18 out of 73 State Guard companies were armed with either rifles or rifle-muskets, while the remainder mostly carried muskets. On June 4, 1861, the Louisville *Weekly Journal* reported that the Glasgow Guards, of Barren County, were in possession of "eighty good muskets belonging to the state." The Thomas Zouaves (aka Louisville Zouaves), commanded by Capt Thomas W. Thompson, received "80 Rifles" via the same source. Other companies in receipt of state arms included the Helm Guards, "80 Enfield Rifles"; the Bullitt Rifles, "80 Austrian rifles & Accoutrements"; the States Company, of Nicholasville, "60 Belgium Rifles"; the Hanley Company, of the same community, "60 Ballard Musketoons"; and the Madison Guards, "60 Muskets."

Of the mounted companies, the Foxtown Rangers of Jackson County and the Elkhorn Rangers of Fayette County both received "Ballard Carbines." On June 17, 1861, Capt DeWitt White, commanding the Silver Creek Rangers of Madison County, reported being in receipt of "44 Sabers, 44 Carbines, [&] 88 Pistols with Accoutrements."

Private Charles B. Mitchell, Co. C, 9th Kentucky Infantry (Caldwell's), wears a tricorn hat pinned up on the sides with a small five-point metal star. His plain gray frock coat is fastened by eight buttons, while his matching gray trousers have broad dark-colored seam stripes. He has a pair of M1851 Colt revolvers pushed into his waist belt, and holds what appears to be a photograph case or small book. Part of the "Orphan Brigade," his regiment fought at Chickamauga and participated in the Atlanta campaign. (William Dunniway collection, USAMHI)

A request issued by the Military Board on July 9, 1861, for the return of all weapons in the hands of the State Guard was ignored by Governor Beriah Magoffin. Commanding the Armstrong Guards, of Louisville, Capt James G. Gorsuch was arrested by Union supporters during August, 1861, for "removing the guns of his company southward."

Of the Kentuckians who volunteered for Confederate service, the 1st Kentucky Battalion (Duncan's) left Louisville unarmed at the end of April 1861. Passing through Nashville, they arrived at Harpers Ferry on May 5, where they requested arms. Evidently this unit was furnished, at least in part, with some of the Harpers Ferry M1841 rifles that had survived the burning of the arsenal; they also received saber bayonets for 211 of these weapons by February 1862.

According to a press report published on August 27, 1861, the two Kentucky regiments forming at Camps Boone and Burnett were to receive "5,000 stand of arms of the most approved and appropriate pattern." In fact these units were furnished with outdated flintlock muskets, Belgian rifles, and even civilian hunting rifles and shotguns. Colonel Tilghman's 3rd and Col Robert P. Trabue's 4th Kentucky Infantry regiments were given 1,000 Virginia Manufactory flintlock muskets via the Ordnance Bureau in Richmond, Virginia. According to Pvt Louis Douglass Payne, Co B, 2nd Kentucky Infantry, "We were armed with old flintlock guns, loading with three small and one large ball, very deadly, but not carrying far" (aka "buck & ball," which increased the chances of hitting a target with a smoothbore musket). The 5th Kentucky Infantry

(Hawkins') received 40 muskets from the same source on October 9, 1861. The scarcity of proper arms for Kentucky regiments was not completely alleviated until the battle of Shiloh in April 1862, when the poorly armed parts of the 6th and 9th Kentucky Regts armed themselves with Enfield rifle-muskets captured from the Federals at the Hornets Nest.

According to Sgt E. Tarrant, Cos A, B, and C, 1st Kentucky Cavalry, were armed with "the Army Sharpe rifles with saber bayonets, one of the most effective arms in the service, and specially adapted to the dragoon or heavy Cavalry service." The other companies of this regiment were afterward armed with "the musket, a very inefficient arm, and particularly inconvenient for Cavalry."

As for the retail supply of arms, at Louisville both Joseph Griffith and Dickson & Gilmore were importers of "Guns, Rifles, Pistols," but it is not known if they supplied military companies of secessionist persuasion. Likewise, dealers Thomas Bradley & Company, at Lexington, sold "Guns, Pistols [&] Bowie Knives." Gilliss & Harney, of the latter city, advertised "42 Double Barreled Guns," and advised those in want of such arms that they had "better call soon." W.W. Meglone, a gunsmith at Limestone Street in Lexington, altered shotguns with "sling strap for Cavalry purposes." Myer & Linz, of Louisville, made Confederate copies of the M1840 cavalry sword, while R.E. Miles produced "military equipments, saddles, knapsacks, cartridge boxes, cap boxes, belts, scabbards, [&] holsters."

According to Kentucky State Guard Special Order No.120, John M. Stokes & Son, at 535 Main Street, Louisville, was contracted to make "knapsacks and other articles." A subsequent order stipulated that 1,000 knapsacks should be made, and that they should be "like those of the Citizen Guards of Louisville." Photographic evidence indicates that these were of the rigid, black leather, militia type with two blanket straps on top and two carrying straps attached to the upper front. In the case of the Citizen Guard, the letters "CG" were painted on the outer rear flap. During the same period contracts were issued for "1,000 haversacks ... after the model in the Inspector General office," and 1,000 "black leather body belts," plus an equal number of mess pans and field kettles. Typical of accoutrements supplied by the state to units of the Kentucky State Guard in 1861 were those received on April 26 by the Preston Greys of Louisville, which comprised 60 each of cartridge box belts, cap boxes and knapsacks, plus one bayonet scabbard. On May 27, the Washington Riflemen of the same city received 42 each of waist belts and plates, knapsacks, and cap boxes. Obviously already well equipped, all the Louisville Life Guards received on May 21 was "40 knapsacks."

Pro-Southern members of the Kentucky State Guard found great difficulty in taking their equipment with them when they removed to Confederate soil. The 21-year-old John W. Green, who enlisted in Co E, 5th Kentucky Infantry (Williams'), recalled that the Citizen Guards of Louisville "loaded their equipments into a farm wagon, threw some straw over them, & then on top of that threw stable manure, & a member of their company dressed as a countryman hauled the equipments through the Federal lines while the other boys Scattered & made their way as best they could to Muldraugh's hill where they found the wagon & their equipments waiting for them."

John T. Hawkins, a private of Co A, 5th Kentucky Cavalry, appears to wear little resembling a uniform, although his hat and boots may have been of military origin. Mainly operating on "foreign soil," most Kentuckians were grateful for whatever clothing they could find. (USAMHI)

(continued on page 33)

MISSOURI VOLUNTEER MILITIA, 1861
1: Officer, Emmet Guards
2: St Louis National Guard
3: 2nd Regiment, (Minute Men)

MISSOURI STATE GUARD, 1861–62
1: Moniteau County Rangers
2: Officer, Campbell's Mounted Company
3: California Guards

B

MISSOURI GUERRILLAS, 1861–64
1: Quantrill's Company, Missouri Infantry (Mounted)
2: Chief scout, Quantrill's Company
3: Guerrilla, Quantrill's Company

C

D

KENTUCKY STATE GUARD, 1861
1: Co A, 4th Kentucky Infantry
2: Sergeant-major
3: Major-general

E

KENTUCKY CAVALRY, 1861–63
1: Lieutenant-colonel, 7th Kentucky Cavalry
2: Co D, 2nd Kentucky Cavalry
3: Co F, 2nd Kentucky Cavalry

F

MARYLAND VOLUNTEER MILITIA, 1861
1: Baltimore City Guard, full dress
2: Maryland Guard Bn, 53rd MVM, undress
3 & 4: Maryland Guard Bn, full dress

G

H

MARYLAND

As a border slave state Maryland was in a very difficult position when the Civil War began. Inhabitants of the low country around the Chesapeake Bay or Eastern Shore tended to sympathize with the South, while many upland Marylanders of German origin, living in the western part of the state, declared for the North. Meanwhile, secessionists outside her borders had struggled for many years to align the state with the South, whilst others sought to keep her in the Union. Although Maryland did not secede in 1861, at least 12,000 volunteers from that state went south to enlist in the Confederate armies.

Antebellum militia

In 1860 the most active element of the militia system of Maryland existed in Baltimore, where the First Light Division of "Maryland Volunteers" was composed entirely of uniformed volunteer militia companies. Within this organization, the 1st Light Brigade consisted of the 1st Cavalry, 1st Artillery and 5th Infantry; the 2nd Brigade boasted the 1st Rifle Regiment, 53rd Infantry (composed of the Independent Greys and the six companies of the Maryland Guard), and the Battalion of Baltimore City Guards. The militia regiments elsewhere in the state existed as enrolled companies on paper only, with uniformed volunteer companies attached either as light infantry, riflemen, cavalry or artillery.

Marylanders became involved in the gathering storm which eventually led to civil war when six companies of volunteer militia from the cities of Baltimore and Frederick – the City Guard, Law Greys, and Shields Guard from the former city, and United Guards, Junior Defenders, and Independent Riflemen from the latter – were involved in putting down the John Brown insurrection during October 1859.

Although no dress regulations were published during the 1850s, the higher ranking officers of the Maryland militia wore a dark blue uniform which closely followed US Army regulations for 1857, the only distinctions apparent being the use of the letters "MM" instead of "US" on hats and caps. Individual volunteer militia companies were permitted to choose distinctive uniforms and wore the usual varieties of patterns and designs. Established in 1857 under Capt Joseph P. Warner, the Baltimore City Guard were reported by the Louisville *Daily Courier* of Kentucky to be wearing "Blue coats and pants, and plume" when they paraded on the Fourth of July of that year. By 1861 the enlisted men of this unit (see Plate G1) wore bearskins "taller than those of the Grenadier Guards," dark blue tail-coats laced with gold, and light blue pants. Officers wore the

This woodblock engraving from *Ballou's Pictorial Drawing-Room Companion,* based on a sketch by Alfred Waud, depicts the full dress parade of the Baltimore City Guard through Charlestown in 1859. Note the variation in headgear, with officers wearing 1851 dress caps, enlisted men in bearskins, and cadets distinguished by a smaller busby. (Anne S.K. Brown Military Collection, Brown University)

same with M1851 dress caps and either pompon or egret plume. Cadets, or junior members, wore smaller black fur busbies with side plumes. The Flank Company of the 53rd Regt – the Independent Greys, commanded by Capt James O. Law – wore gray tailcoats trimmed black, dress caps with white fountain plumes, and white summer pants. Formed in December 1859, the Maryland Guard Battalion of Baltimore City (see Plates G2–G4) adopted four combinations of uniform. Their Class A outfit consisted of "Full Chasseur uniform, without overcoat; White belts; Knapsack." Class B dress included a "Fatigue Jacket; Chasseur pants; Overcoat without cape." Class C was the same as B, but with caped overcoat, and Class D comprised a "Fatigue Jacket; Dark pants; Black belts." On the occasion of the visit of the Japanese Embassy party to Baltimore on June 7, 1860, the Maryland Guard were ordered to appear in "A fatigue Cap and jacket, plain white pants, with suspenders, white cotton gloves, black stock, without collar, thick shoes or boots neatly polished, and a black leather belt of the adopted pattern." Constituting the remainder of the 5th and 53rd Infantry, companies such as the Law Grays, German Guards, and National Blues also wore distinctive uniforms of their own choice.

In Anne Arundel County the newly formed Magothy Home Guard had their full dress uniforms made by Patterson and Fields, of Baltimore, which was described in the Baltimore *Sun* of February 21, 1861, as consisting of a coat "of fine blue cloth, heavily trimmed with gold lace, with pants of the same material and color, ornamented with a broad stripe of orange upon the outer seams." The Patuxent Mounted Guard of Patuxent City, Charles County, acquired a complete set of uniforms produced "at the establishment of Mr Thomas McCormick, Carroll Hall" in Baltimore. Their coats were of "fine blue cloth, heavily trimmed with gold lace, with pants of the same material and color, ornamented with a broad stripe of orange upon the outer seams." Organized at Carrollton Manor in Frederick County during 1859, the Manor Mounted Guard bore on their tall dress caps the letters "MMG" under an 1851 pompon, eagle and fountain plume; their dark blue coats had high-standing collars, small militia-style epaulettes, and two rows of trim around the cuffs. Attached to the 3rd Regt, Maryland Militia, the Mounted Guard of Montgomery County wore M1858 dress hats with black plume and yellow hat cord, plus "crossed sabers" with points down over the letters "MMG." Their dark blue frock coats were trimmed yellow around collar and pointed cuffs, and were embellished with brass shoulder scales. Trousers were medium blue with yellow seam stripes. Situated along the Virginia state line, many members of this company slipped across the border and joined the Confederate army.

Prior to the Civil War, William H. Murray commanded Co D, Maryland Guard Battalion, a volunteer militia unit organized in 1859. Most of this unit enlisted in Confederate service as Co H, 1st Maryland Infantry on June 21, 1861. Murray wears the antebellum uniform of an officer of the Maryland Guard, which included a sky-blue chasseur-style cap with dark blue band and narrow yellow cord trim, and a plain nine-button frock coat with Federal-style shoulder straps. (Dave Mark Collection)

Maryland volunteers

With news of the secession of Virginia, and Lincoln's call for Northern troops to suppress the Southern "rebellion," approximately 15,000 Marylanders enrolled under the command of Col Isaac R. Trimble on April 20, 1861, for the defense of Baltimore. These recruits were organized into three regiments of citizen militia: the Maryland Line, the Southern Guerrilla Home Guard, and a regiment composed of volunteer militia, the latter being commanded by Trimble himself. Originally used by the Maryland Continental Troops in the American Revolutionary War of 1775–83, and sometimes referred to as the "Old Line," the "Maryland Line" had been regarded by George Washington as among his finest soldiers, and Marylanders subsequently volunteering for Confederate service proudly revived the name. The Maryland Line established by Trimble in Baltimore in April 1861 consisted of the Naval Harbor Marines, a 75-man unit crewing four gunboats, plus nine two-company battalions of infantry; the various companies wore gray Garibaldi shirts, black pants, and glazed caps. As far as is known the Southern Guerrilla Home Guard was composed of only one battalion of four companies, and was to be used to ambush and harry advancing Union columns. Trimble's own Volunteer Regiment contained a staggering 33 companies; it included units such as the Canton Light Infantry, Baltimore Home Guard and Maryland Chasseurs, who presumably wore various styles of fatigue dress. The Maryland Duckers, commanded by Capt William McDonald, wore "a drab shirt and pants and slouch hat bearing the coat of arms of Maryland."

When Federal forces under Gen Benjamin Butler occupied Baltimore, these units were forbidden to assemble and ceased to function. However, many of their members, as well as pro-Southern supporters from all other

Entitled "Camp Johnson, near Winchester, Virginia – The First Maryland Regiment playing foot-ball before evening parade," this engraving was published in *Harper's Weekly* on August 31, 1861, and shows the Marylanders wearing the uniforms they received during May–June 1861. (Author's collection)

After joining the company of Marylanders recruited in Richmond, VA, by Capt Murray, John T. Bond subsequently enlisted in Co H, 1st Maryland Infantry in June 1861. The black tape trim across his chest indicates that he served as a musician. (USAMHI)

parts of the state, stole out of the city and made for Virginia singly, in small groups, or even by companies. By early May about 500 volunteers from various locations in Maryland were gathered under Capt Bradley T. Johnson at Points of Rock and Harpers Ferry, where they were organized into eight companies of Maryland infantry.

Meanwhile, members of the élite volunteer militia of Baltimore, such as the Maryland Guard and Independent Greys, regarded themselves as superior to the battalion Johnson was organizing at Harpers Ferry. Proceeding to Richmond, they offered their services to the Virginia authorities. As a result, the Marylanders were to be enlisted into three regiments and mustered into the service of Virginia. In carrying out this plan Governor John Letcher of Virginia issued commissions to Francis J. Thomas, an ex-captain in the US Army, as colonel of the 1st Regt; Bradley T. Johnson was to be lieutenant-colonel of the 2nd Regt, while Alden Weston would be major of the 3rd; if three regiments failed to emerge, the volunteers that remained would be consolidated into one unit under these officers. However, Johnson declined his commission, refusing to enter the military service of Virginia on the grounds that Maryland must be represented by Maryland regiments. Consequently, he had the eight Harpers Ferry companies mustered into the army of the Confederate States rather than that of Virginia, and urged the consolidation of all Marylanders who served the Confederacy.

In the meantime, the ex-Baltimoreans at Richmond were received by Col Thomas and organized into a battalion under Maj Weston. Formerly a lieutenant in the Baltimore City Guard, Edward R. Dorsey was elected to command the Weston Guards on May 16, 1861. Known as the Maryland Guards, two further companies were organized under captains William H. Murray and J. Lyle Clarke. A fourth company, composed of recruits from St Mary's, Calvert and Charles counties, was led by Capt Michael S. Robertson. Shortly after this, Clarke's company enlisted for twelve months as Co B, 21st Virginia Infantry, and served in the Army of Northern Virginia until May 1862. The other three companies were united with Johnson's battalion at Harpers Ferry on June 25, 1861. Reorganized into six companies, Johnson's command became the 1st Maryland Infantry, with Col Arnold Elzey in command. This unit fought at First Manassas, in Jackson's Valley Campaign, and the Seven Days' Battles, before disbanding in August 1862. Lieutenant-Colonel George H. Steuart and Maj B.T. Johnson continued their efforts to organize Marylanders fighting for the Confederacy into the "Maryland Line," which was finally authorized on June 22, 1863, by Secretary of War James A. Seddon.

Upon arrival at Richmond, the Baltimoreans were initially advised to furnish their "own blankets and clothing." The eight Harpers Ferry companies were also poorly clad, although "the ladies of Baltimore" managed to smuggle some uniforms and side-arms through the Union lines concealed under the hoops of their dresses. According to a correspondent of the *Daily Dispatch* of Richmond, the cloth for one officer's uniform had been basted together and worn as "an under-garment" for the same purpose. This remained the situation until these companies were amalgamated with the three from Richmond at Winchester, Virginia, in June 1861.

On or about May 20, 1861, the Richmond-based companies acquired uniforms from Kent, Paine and Co of 163–165 Main Street in that city. Described as being of "coarse grey, but very durable," that worn by Pvt E. Courtney Jenkins, of J. Lyle Clarke's company, survives in the Museum of the Confederacy, and consists of a six-button shell jacket and trousers made of heavy satinette. The jacket collar and shoulder straps, and trouser outer seams, are bound in half-inch black tape; narrow gray tape belt loops are attached near the jacket side seams.

Meanwhile, Jane Claudia Johnson, wife of the major of the 1st Maryland (Elzey's) and a native of North Carolina, raised about $10,000 among "enthusiastic North Carolinians and Virginians," and "secured cloth ... by purchasing it from the mills where it was manufactured for the State of Virginia, and ... paid for making it up into uniforms." Thus by the beginning of July, 1861, the 1st Maryland was supplied with uniforms consisting of "a French kepi (a little gray cap), a natty gray roundabout, collar and sleeves bound with black braid, and a similar stripe down the gray trousers." This uniform was in all probability patterned on those made by Kent, Paine & Co for the Richmond-based Maryland companies. Non-commissioned officers wore their black chevrons point down on their right sleeves only.

Maryland zouaves

Several companies of pro-Confederate zouaves were recruited in Maryland during 1861 due to the influence of Richard Thomas, a native of St Mary's County on the southern border with Virginia. Born in 1833, he was the son of Richard Thomas, Sr, former president of the Maryland Senate and brother of Governor James Thomas of Maryland. Richard Thomas was educated at the Charlotte Hall Academy, a military boarding school, and briefly at the US Military Academy, from which he resigned in 1851. He spent some time working on government surveys of California and other western territories, and as a soldier of fortune fighting river pirates in China. He was also among a number of Americans who journeyed to Italy to fight alongside Garibaldi in the struggle for Italian independence against the Hapsburg empire. It was during the latter campaign that he adopted the military rank and name of "Colonel Richard Thomas Zarvona," by which title he was known thereafter.

Cpl Francis Higdon, Co I, 1st Maryland Infantry wears an example of the "coarse grey" uniform with trim around collar and shoulder straps supplied by Kent, Paine & Co of Richmond, VA, to the four companies of Maryland volunteers raised in that city. It is not known whether his Corsican-style cap was supplied to the whole company or was headgear specific to Higdon – see Plate H3. In this reversed image his two narrow, close-set rank chevrons appear on his left rather than his right sleeve. (Tom Clemens Collection, USAMHI)

Thirteen-year-old William Dorsey Skinner enlisted in Co C, 2nd Maryland Infantry Battalion, on September 19, 1862. His cap bears a large wreath with indistinguishable letters which probably indicate his regiment and company. His unusually trimmed shell jacket has three buttons on the front of each cuff, and his trousers have broad light-colored seam stripes. (USAMHI)

An ardent secessionist, Thomas joined with others, including George W. Alexander and William C. Walters, to form two infantry companies in St Mary's and Calvert counties, Maryland, to be drilled as "Zouaves for the Confederate service," and to be known as the Maryland Zouaves. On June 28, 1861, Zarvona became a national hero of the Confederacy when, dressed as a "French lady," he captured a Chesapeake Bay steamer, the *St Nicholas*, and went on to take three Federal merchant vessels. The Confederate authorities at Fredericksburg honored the action of the "Potomac Zouaves," and Governor Letcher of Virginia commissioned Zarvona a colonel in the state forces.

Zarvona was described in the Richmond press on July 6, 1861, as presenting "a picturesque appearance, attired in his blue Zouave costume, white gaiters, red cap with gold tassel and light elegant sword." In a later account published in the *Confederate Veteran* magazine in 1914, ex-Governor John Letcher of Virginia stated that Zarvona wore "the zouave dress and cap corresponding with it. His hair was cut very close." A red fez with a dark blue tassel, attributed to Zarvona, survives today in the collection of the Maryland Historical Society. Presumably the Maryland Zouaves donned a uniform based on what their commanding officer wore.

By early July 1861, plans were under way to organize the Maryland Zouaves, 1st Regt, with William Walters in command of the "first company," and Thomas Blackistone commanding the "second company." Meanwhile, Zarvona became involved in further naval escapades on Chesapeake Bay; captured, and imprisoned for two years in a Federal prison, he was finally freed in April 1863 on the understanding that he would live abroad until the war was over. After a prolonged stay in Paris, France, he returned to Maryland where he died in 1875.

Meanwhile the Maryland Zouaves, 1st Regt, failed to materialize and the Zouave company led by Walters was designated Co H, 47th Virginia Infantry, while Blackistone's company were detailed as guards at the Castle Thunder Prison in Richmond. After service on the Peninsula, Walter's company was transferred to the 2nd Arkansas Bn, and was mustered out of service on June 10, 1862. On January 8 of that year, Walters' company received a box of 57 overcoats of unknown pattern; this is one of the largest numbers of overcoats requisitioned at one time by a Confederate infantry company.

Later in 1862 Louis Keepers was elected to command the Guerrilla Zouaves. Organized in Richmond and composed mainly of Marylanders, this unit was assigned to the 1st Louisiana Infantry (Nelligan's) as the second Company C. It is doubtful that this company wore a zouave-style uniform.

Military suppliers

As the wealthiest and most prized seaport in the state, Baltimore was the center for military supply in Maryland, and smugglers continued to ship Baltimore-made goods across Chesapeake Bay to Virginia throughout the conflict. Military cloth could be had in Baltimore at Wethered Brothers, on German Street. On January 22, 1861, Charles and John Wethered stated in the Baltimore *Sun* that they had "on hand and are manufacturing every description of Cloths suitable for military purposes." Whiteley, Stone & Company, of the same city, advertised "Fulled Cloth for Uniforms ... Gray and other colors, suitable for Uniforms." This firm also advised that they had "Blankets, Shirts, etc. for the Troops ... suitable for military purposes," and of the same styles and qualities as they were furnishing to the city of Baltimore by contract, which indicates that they were main suppliers to the city militia.

The Lanier Guards were organized and equipped in Baltimore by George Lanier of Lanier Brothers, wholesale and dry goods merchants. This company adopted a plan to slip out of the city unnoticed under cover of a funeral procession to Loudon Park Cemetery. Once there, the coffin containing their guns and accoutrements was unpacked and the equipment re-issued. This unit became Co G, 13th Virginia Infantry.

Headgear was supplied by Joseph Bernhard, who stated in the local press that his store at 208 West Pratt Street, Baltimore, was the "only place where Military Hats and Caps are made to please, and at the shortest notice." Uniforms were produced by tailors John H. Rea & Company, suppliers to "the Maryland Light Division Volunteers," who were prepared to "manufacture Uniforms for Military Companies in any quantity." Other Baltimore-based military tailors included John Mullen and Thomas McCormick. A general purveyor of military goods, Charles Sisco produced "Military Trimmings of every description" including "Gold and Silver Fringes, Laces, Cords, Tassels, Stars, Edgings, Braids, Bouillon [sic] Spangles" plus "Guidons for Troop, Companies, &c. Banners."

Belt plates and buttons worn by Maryland militia and Confederate volunteers bore a modified version of the reverse of the seal of the Lords of Baltimore. This consisted of a shield inscribed with the quartered arms of the Calvert and Crossland families surmounted by an eagle. The Calvert portion of the arms showed six vertical bands intersected by a diagonal stripe, while those of the Crossland family were represented by a Greek cross with arms ending in trefoils. Written on the scroll under the shield was the Latin motto *Crescite et Multiplicimini*, meaning "increase and multiply." Supporters either side of the shield consist of a farmer and a fisherman.

James W. Jenkins, Jr, served in Co E, 1st Maryland Cavalry, until his capture near Hagerstown on July 6, 1863, while guarding a supply train retreating from Gettysburg. He wears a double-breasted frock coat with trim on the cuffs, and has balanced his light-colored felt hat on the photographer's table. (Dave Mark Collection)

Sword belt plates with round interlocking tongue and wreath bearing this device were produced by James S. Smith of New York City. Oval waist belt and cartridge box plates were furnished by Emerson Gaylord, at Chicopee, Massachusetts. Shortly before the war some of Baltimore's uniformed companies purchased from the latter firm a quantity of sword belts with rectangular plates bearing these arms. The large Baltimore store of Canfield, Brother & Co supplied numerous uniform buttons bearing this device before the Civil War. Jacob Gminder, on Calvert Street, Baltimore, supplied buttons made by the Scovill Manufacturing Company at Waterbury, Connecticut. Other Northern firms producing buttons of this pattern included Fitch and Waldo of New York. Over 50 Confederate infantry block-I buttons, plus metal civilian buttons with the back marks "Hinds Balto" and "W.O. Linthicum Balt. Md.," were dug up at the camp of the 1st Maryland where the Harpers Ferry and Richmond companies were united on June 24, 1861. The former were perhaps deliberately cut off their uniforms and replaced by Maryland state seal buttons.

Several manufacturers and importers of musical instruments in Baltimore probably supplied drums and bugles that were carried to Virginia for Confederate use. William Boucher, Jr, and the Eisenbrandt family produced drums with very distinctive "eagle" designs. The 1st Maryland Infantry (Steuart's) was issued 10 drums and two bugles via the C.S. Quartermaster Department. The instrument carried by Drum Major Hosea Pitt of that regiment survives today in the Confederate Room of the Maryland Historical Society, but does not have a maker's label. During March 1862, when they relieved the 13th Virginia on picket duty west of Sangster's Station, Virginia, the Marylanders were attacked by a body of Union cavalry. One drummer abandoned his instrument and fled, only to be stopped by Col Steuart, who demanded to know where his instrument was. Turning to Drum Major Pitt, he exclaimed, "It's a good thing that I have not yet had the Maryland flag painted on the drums."

Arms and equipage

Following their involvement in quelling the John Brown insurrection in 1859, the Independent Greys of Baltimore were reported in the *Daily Enquirer*, of Richmond, to have been presented with "a Sharp's rifle each from those captured at Harpers Ferry." The Frederick Mounted Dragoons commanded by Capt Bradley Johnson were armed with "Hall's carbines, an antiquated and rejected breechloader," upon their return from Baltimore in April 1861. These arms were possibly part of the "500 Hall carbines for Cavalry service and 2000 Hall carbines with sliding or ramrod bayonets" advertised by Francis W. Bennett, on Charles Street, Baltimore, during November 1860 through January 1861.

Volunteer militia companies organizing in the wake of the John Brown insurrection received various arms from the state. On June 14, 1860,

This unidentified Maryland cavalryman wears a jacket fastened by nine small ball buttons, and sports large leather gauntlets, with two holstered revolvers attached to his waist belt. (USAMHI)

the Smallwood Riflemen of Charles County, attached to the 1st Regt, Maryland Militia, received 50 Minie rifles and accoutrements. Commanded by Capt Herman Stump, the Harford Riflemen, 40th Regt, were issued 50 rifled muskets and accoutrements in September 1860. In Anne Arundel County, the Patapsco Light Dragoons, 3rd Regt, obtained 40 sabers, pistols and accoutrements on February 20, 1861.

Organized towards the end of April 1861, the Maryland Line militia were issued with 150 rifle-muskets, 250 smoothbore muskets, and 2,000 pikes made at the factory of Baltimore-based railroad engineer and inventor Ross Winans. Doubtless, the workmen from his shops who enlisted for service as the Winans Guard – Co J, 5th Infantry, Maryland Militia – were armed with these weapons. The Maryland Duckers of Trimble's regiment were armed with "large double barrelled fowling pieces, revolvers and Bowie knives."

On April 20, 1861, following the riots in Baltimore provoked by the arrival of the 6th Massachusetts on its way to the Federal capital, Capt Wilson C. Nicholas, commanding the Garrison Forest Rangers, 45th Regt, Maryland Militia (afterwards Co G, 1st Maryland Infantry) seized the US arsenal at Pikesville, where there was a deposit of antiquated arms and a considerable supply of gunpowder.

On June 3, 1861, Johnson's battalion at Harpers Ferry received "Five Hundred Mississippi rifles (cal. 54), Ten Thousand cartridges, and Thirty-five Hundred caps," due to the efforts of Jane Claudia Johnson, wife of Col Bradley Johnson, who travelled under escort to her home state to acquire these arms from Governor John Ellis of North Carolina. An invoice of the Ordnance Department states that "500 rifles made at Herkimer NY without bayonets" were issued to Mrs Johnson. The 220 men of the three Richmond companies who joined Johnson carried M1842 Springfield smoothbore muskets and bayonets. William E. Colston was a private in J. Lyle Clarke's company, which enlisted as Co B, 21st Virginia Infantry, on May 23, 1861; he wrote: "My musket being the only one brought from Baltimore that I know of [,] it is still an object of attention. Our company is armed with flintlocks altered to percussion."

On August 28, the Maryland Zouaves commanded by Zarvona received black waist belts and bayonet scabbards. Two Richmond-based firms, Robert Hough & Co and Meredith Spencer & Co, formerly of Baltimore, supplied accoutrements for several Maryland companies in Confederate service. Saddle, harness, and collar manufacturer E.W. Briding had "Military Equipments for Cavalry Troops made at the shortest notice and lowest terms," at West Pratt Street in Baltimore. During April 1861, Cortlan & Company, of Baltimore, sold "Camp Military Goods," including knives, forks, spoons, china plates, cooking utensils, and tin cups.

Capt James McHenry Howard (left), 1st Maryland Infantry, and his brother David Ridgely Howard, Co A, 2nd Maryland Infantry, were photographed in Canada in their Confederate uniforms at the war's end. David has a metal "cross bottony" pinned to his breast, which is believed to have been the insignia of the Maryland Line – see Plate H2. (Dave Mark Collection)

SELECT BIBLIOGRAPHY

Anderson, Ephraim McD., *Memoirs: Historical and Personal; including the Campaigns of the First Missouri Brigade* (St Louis, Times Printing Co, 1868)

Bazelon, Bruce B., & William F. McGuinn, *A Directory of American Military Goods Dealers & Makers 1785–1885* (REF Typesetting & Publishing Inc, Manassas, VA, 1987)

Crouch, Howard R., *Horse Equipment of the Civil War Era* (Fairfax, VA, 2003)

Dorsey, R. Stephen, & Kenneth L. McPheeters, *The American Military Saddle, 1776–1945* (Eugene, OR, 1999)

Farthing, C.M., *Chronicles of the Civil War in Monroe County* (n.p., n.d.)

Field, Ron, *American Civil War: Confederate Army* (Brasseys, London, 1996)

Goldsborough, William Worthington, *The Maryland Line in the Confederate Army* (January 1994)

Hartzler, Daniel D., *Arms Makers of Maryland* (George Shumway, York PA, 1977)

Hartzler, Daniel D., *Marylanders in the Confederacy* (Family Line Publishers, Silver Spring MD, 1986)

Hartzler, Daniel D., *A Band of Brothers: Photographic Epilogue to Marylanders in the Confederacy* (Heritage Books, New Windsor MD, 2005)

Hyde, William, & H.L. Conrad, *Encyclopedia of the History of St Louis*, 4 vols. (New York & Louisville KY, 1899)

Lane, Peter D., *Recollections of a Volunteer or Footsteps of a Soldier* (Honey Creek Township, Henry County MO, 1865)

McGhee, James E., *Missouri Confederates: A Guide to Sources for Confederate Soldiers and Units, 1861–1865* (Two Trails Publishing, Independence MO, 2001)

Manakee, Harold R., *Maryland in the Civil War* (Maryland Historical Society, 1961)

Meekus, George A. *Fifth Regiment, Infantry, Maryland National Guard: History of the Regiment from Its First Organization to the Present Time* (Baltimore, 1889)

Mudd, Joseph A., *With Porter in North Missouri: A Chapter in the History of the War Between the States* (National Publishing Company, Washington DC, 1909)

Mullinax, Steve E., *Confederate Belt Buckles & Plates* (Alexandria VA, 1999)

Murphy, John, & Howard Michael Madaus, *Confederate Rifles & Muskets* (Graphics Publishers, 1996)

Nicholson, Isaac F. "The Maryland Guard Battalion, 1860–1861" in *Maryland Historical Magazine* (6 June 1911)

O'Donnell, Michael J., & J. Duncan Campbell, *American Military Belt Plates* (Alexandria VA, 1996)

Stone, Jr., Richard G., *A Brittle Sword: The Kentucky Militia, 1776–1912* (University Press of Kentucky, Lexington, 1977)

Tarrant, Eastham, *The wild riders of the First Kentucky cavalry* (Press of R.H. Carothers, Louisville, c.1894)

Tice, Warren K., *Uniform Buttons of the United States, 1776–1865* (Gettysburg, 1997)

Todd, Frederick P., *American Military Equipage 1851–1872*, Vol.I (The Company of Military Historians, 1974)

Todd, Frederick P., *American Military Equipage 1851–1872*, Vol.II, "State Forces" (Chatham Square Press, 1983)

Plus various contemporary newspapers.

PLATE COMMENTARIES

A: MISSOURI VOLUNTEER MILITIA, 1861

The officer of the **Emmet Guards (A1)** wears full dress, including an 1847 pattern black beaver chapeau de bras with "high hump" shape, as introduced by the US Army in 1832. His dark blue double-breasted frock coat has buff-colored facings on collar and cuffs, and is fastened with two rows of seven brass Missouri state seal buttons. His sky-blue trousers have buff seam stripes. He is armed with an M1850 Foot Officer's sword in a metal scabbard, suspended from a black leather sword belt fastened with an 1851 pattern "eagle" plate.

The private of the **St Louis National Guard (A2)** wears an 1855 pattern black felt "National Guard"-style dress cap with 1851 "eagle" plate and brass wreath with letter "A" inset, surmounted by a white wool pompon. His dark blue single-breasted frock coat has brass shoulder scales attached, and is fastened with nine brass buttons, plus two small buttons behind each cuff. His sky-blue trousers have white seam stripes. His whitened buff leather waist belt has a brass plate bearing the initials "MVM" and supports a black leather cap pouch. An 1839 pattern plate with monogram "NG" is attached to his shoulder belts, from which are suspended a black leather cartridge box and a black leather bayonet scabbard in a white leather frog. He is armed with an M1842 percussion smoothbore musket.

The enlisted man, **2nd Regiment, Missouri Volunteer Militia (Minute Men) (A3)** wears a short dark gray jacket, edged and embellished with black braid in an approximation of zouave style, and matching trousers with black seam stripes. Headgear is a mid-gray forage cap with a black top surface to the crown. A black leather waist belt fastened with an oval brass plate bearing the initials "MVM" supports a black leather cap pouch and bayonet scabbard. His black leather cartridge box hangs from a shoulder belt worn under his jacket, displaying an "eagle" plate. He carries a .69cal M1816 conversion musket with fixed socket bayonet.

The Duval brothers, Pvt Thomas Duval (left) and Lt William Duval (right), served originally in the Missouri State Guard before joining the 3rd Missouri Infantry. They both wear homemade fatigue shirts with light-colored trimming, reminiscent of 1821 state regulations – compare with Plate B1. Note the secession cockade pinning up Thomas Duval's hat brim. (Courtesy Wilson's Creek National Battlefield)

B: MISSOURI STATE GUARD, 1861–62

The enlisted man of the **Moniteau County Rangers (B1)** wears an oilcloth-covered cap with "MR" painted in white at the front. His gray flannel pullover shirt, fastened with four small bone buttons, is trimmed around the collar, chest, pockets, and cuffs with yellow braid, and his gray cassimere pantaloons have yellow seam stripes. Footwear consists of 1851 pattern Jefferson brogans. His brown leather waist belt, with a forked-tongue buckle, supports a black leather cap pouch. An 1839 pattern black leather cartridge box is suspended from a leather sling with an "eagle" breast plate. A tarred cloth haversack is slung on his left hip, and he has an 1858 canteen with tan-colored cloth cover. He is armed with an M1816 musket converted to percussion and shortened for use as a cavalry carbine.

Based on photographic evidence, the officer of **Campbell's Mounted Company (B2)** wears a black felt hat looped up on one side with a coat-sized gilt military button, and sports a black ostrich feather plume. His gray flannel shirt has narrow mid-blue trim around the stand-and-fall collar and cuffs, and solid mid-blue trim on the placket front and V-shaped pocket tops. He carries an infantry officer's sword with straight blade, mother-of-pearl grip and Indian-head pommel, slung to a dark brown leather sword belt with deep roll-embossing, fastened with a rectangular "eagle" plate.

The enlisted man of the **California Guards (B3)** wears an 1839 pattern dark blue forage cap with rounded black leather visor and chin strap. His striped cotton civilian shirt is fastened with small white bone buttons, as is his double-breasted gray cassimere vest with wide turn-down collar

and lapels. His trousers are of plain butternut-brown jean cloth. Accoutrements consist of an 1820 militia officer's wide leather sword belt with two narrow leather straps to the small brass frame buckles, supporting a black leather cap pouch. A dark brown leather revolver holster is suspended by a loop, and he also has a small bone-handled Bowie knife in a red leather sheath. Behind his right hip an 1839 pattern cartridge box is suspended from a shoulder belt, with the brass oval "US" plate removed from the flap but the round "eagle" breast plate retained. He has shouldered a .69cal converted musket without sling.

C: MISSOURI GUERRILLAS, 1861–64

The enlisted man of **Quantrill's Company, Missouri Infantry (C1)** – in fact, a mounted unit – has a black civilian felt hat with tall pointed crown. His homemade red cotton shirt has yellow trim around the collar, pocket top and n wavy lines down each side of the front opening. His trousers are plain dark blue wool. He holds a Sharps slant-breech carbine, and is equipped with an 1816 pattern black leather waist belt with cast brass frame buckle, with a sheathed Bowie knife suspended from a black leather frog. His ammunition is carried in an 1839 pattern Rifleman's flask and pouch belt suspended over his left shoulder, with a second Bowie knife, complete with brass ring guards (possibly for attachment to a pike staff), secured to the pouch belt by a stud at mid-chest height. He is seated in a brown leather Morgan saddle, minus tree, with bentwood stirrups, over a plaid blanket.

Based on a photograph of George Maddox, the **Chief Scout, Quantrill's Company (C2)**, wears a dark gray felt hat with black and white feathers in its black silk band. His cadet-gray frock coat has pale blue facing color on collar and pointed cuffs, while his red flannel pullover shirt has elaborate dark blue ruffling around its deep V-neck. His trousers are plain light gray wool, worn with knee-high "Napoleon"-style boots and brass spurs. He is armed with two .44cal six-shot Remington Army revolvers; his leather waist belt is converted from a cartridge box shoulder belt with an iron roller buckle, supporting the two holsters (hidden here by his coat). A "horsehead" Bowie knife with brown horn grip, in a red leather sheath, is also attached to the waist belt.

The guerrilla of **Quantrill's Company (C3)**, is based on a photograph of the notorious Jesse James. He wears a small mid-gray low-crowned felt hat with a black silk band and a single black ostrich feather plume. His gray flannel pullover shirt has dark blue trim and small buttons around the deep neck and the pocket top; his trousers are captured Federal-issue plain sky-blue wool, tucked into "Wellington"-style calf boots with brass spurs. He has two Colt Third Model Dragoon revolvers, holstered on a black leather 1851 pattern enlisted man's sword belt with "eagle" plate; his white cotton haversack contains packages of ammunition plus spare revolver cylinders.

D: KENTUCKY VOLUNTEER MILITIA, 1861

The private of the **Citizen Guards (D1)** wears full dress, including a large bearskin with a gold tassel. His cadet-gray tailcoat has a black plastron front with three rows of nine brass buttons linked together by yellow braid; the standing collar and pointed cuffs are faced with black cloth and

Simon Bolivar Buckner in the Kentucky State Guard uniform he designed in 1860 – see Plate E3. Two rows of Kentucky state buttons are arranged in groups of three, in line with 1857 US Army regulations for a major-general. His slash cuffs are fastened with three small buttons. His gray cap with black band and gold braid may be seen at top right, the quatrefoil knot on the crown top just visible. Buckner resigned from command of the State Guard on July 20, 1861, and accepted the rank of brigadier-general in the CS Army. Captured at Fort Donelson in February 1862, he was later exchanged, and went on to command a division and a corps; he lived until January 1914, the last surviving Confederate officer above the rank of brigadier-general. (Author's collection)

edged with yellow braid; small infantry buglehorn devices are embroidered each side of his collar; and note the black-fringed yellow epaulettes. His matching trousers have black seam stripes, edged yellow, and his black leather waist belt, supporting a cap pouch, is fastened with a rectangular brass militia "eagle" plate. His whitened buff shoulder belts, with plain square breast plate, support a socket bayonet in a whitened frog and a black leather cartridge box bearing the brass monogram "CG" on the outer flap. He is armed with an M1842 .69cal Springfield musket. The Citizen Guards enlisted for Confederate service as Co B, 5th/9th Kentucky Infantry, and served throughout the war in the Orphan Brigade.

The enlisted man of the **Lexington Rifles (D2)** wears full dress of an 1851 pattern bottle-green cap with yellow band, "eagle" plate and militia-pattern letters "LR," surmounted by a dark green pompon. His bottle-green frock coat has yellow braid around the collar and cuffs, and attached brass shoulder scales; the gilt metal buttons bear the state coat of arms and motto. His matching trousers have wide yellow seam stripes.

The **Lexington Rifles musician (D3)** wears undress comprising a dark blue 1839 forage cap, and a very loose-fitting gray hunting coat with billowing sleeves, and five pleats either side of the six-button front. His bottle-green trousers are as for full dress. The Lexington Rifles were mounted and became "Morgan's Squadron," later serving in the 2nd Kentucky Cavalry.

The enlisted man of the **National Blues (D4)** wears a dark blue 1858 forage cap with the wreathed white metal letters "NB." His dark blue wool frock coat has a single row of white metal buttons; the collar bears a button and a white braid "blind buttonhole" each side. His 1851 white worsted epaulettes have white wool fringes, and his sky-blue trousers have white seam stripes. Here he wears white cotton dress gloves, and holds an 1816 conversion musket. His whitened buff leather waist belt is fastened with a rectangular brass militia "eagle" plate supporting a black leather cap pouch, and his shoulder belts, with a plain square breast plate, support a socket bayonet in a white frog and a black leather cartridge box bearing brass letters "NB" on the outer flap.

E: KENTUCKY STATE GUARD, 1861

The enlisted man of **Co A, 4th Kentucky Infantry (E1)**, wears a light gray chasseur-style cap with dark blue band and cord trim. His steel-gray frock coat has mid-blue facings on the standing collar, cuffs, and epaulette "bridle" straps. His trousers are plain cadet-gray. He holds a Virginia Manufactory flintlock musket. His brown leather waist belt is fastened with a gilt forked-tongue buckle, and a Rifleman's flask and pouch belt are slung over his left shoulder under the blanket roll wrapped in his gum blanket. A tin militia-style canteen is carried on a white cotton sling. Like the Citizen Guards (D1), the 4th Kentucky also served in the Orphan Brigade.

The **sergeant-major (E2)** wears a cadet-gray uniform consisting of an 1858 forage cap with a black band, an 1851 frock coat with black facings on the shoulder straps, and points-up black rank chevrons on his upper sleeves. His plain cadet-gray trousers are tucked into brown leather buckled gaiters. He has unsheathed an M1840 non-commissioned officer's sword; his dark brown leather militia NCO's sword belt, with integral hanger, is fastened with a two-piece "eagle" plate.

The **major-general in full dress (E3)** is based on photographs of Simon Bolivar Buckner. His light gray chasseur-style forage cap has a black band and gold lace trim, and his cadet-gray frock coat is fastened with a double row of nine gilt buttons bearing the state seal and arranged in groups of three, as per US Army regulations. His collar is faced with black velvet and edged with gold lace, and bears rank

John H. Carter served in John Hunt Morgan's 2nd Kentucky Cavalry – see Plate F2. He holds a locally made and rather primitive-looking saber, and wears a grey frock coat with dark – possibly yellow – trim on the cuffs. A wide-brimmed straw hat rests on his knees. (USAMHI)

insignia for a major-general of the Kentucky State Guard – a silver-embroidered five-point star either side of a silver-embroidered, gold-edged US shield. Note the unusual shoulder straps, faced with black velvet edged with gold lace, with two inner rows of silver lace and a silver spread eagle; the plain black velvet cuff facing is without gold trim. Matching trousers have narrow black seam stripes. He holds a saber with buff leather sword knot; his general officer's sword belt of dark reddish-brown leather, with three gold lace stripes, is fastened with a gilt tongue-and-wreath "eagle" plate.

F: KENTUCKY CAVALRY, 1861–63

The uniform of the lieutenant-colonel, **7th Kentucky Cavalry (F1)** is based on photographs of Col Richard M. Gano. The headgear is a black felt tricorn hat with black silk edging, gold tassel, and black ostrich plume. His cadet-gray frock coat has yellow facings on collar and cuffs, with rank insignia of two gold-embroidered five-point stars on the former, and three buttons on the latter. His dark blue trousers have gold seam stripes. He carries a brass-hilted Foot Officer's sword which he has drawn from a leather scabbard with brass throat, rings, and drag. His black leather waist belt, over a red wool sash, is fastened with a gilt oval plate bearing the state arms.

Based on a photograph of John H. Carter, the trooper of **Co D, 2nd Kentucky Cavalry (F2)**, wears a wide-brimmed straw hat with gray silk band, cadet-gray frock coat with narrow yellow cord trim on the cuffs, and plain lighter gray trousers tucked into brown leather boots. He is dropping a locally-made saber with plain brass hilt and knuckle guard. Both of these regiments took part in Morgan's raid into Ohio and Illinois in 1863.

The trooper, **Co F, 2nd Kentucky Cavalry (F3)** wears a black felt hat with gray silk band, and a light gray shell jacket with a yellow standing collar and yellow facings on the cuffs; these have a long tongue up the back seam with six small "zouave-style" gilt state buttons. Trousers of darker gray are tucked into black leather boots. He brandishes an M1840 Dragoon saber, and has a holstered M1858 Remington-Beals Army percussion revolver on his pale leather sword belt with rectangular gilt "eagle" plate.

G: MARYLAND VOLUNTEER MILITIA

The private of the **Baltimore City Guard (G1)** in full dress wears a black bearskin with gold tassel. His dark blue tailcoat has two rows of ten gilt buttons arranged in pairs, and buttoned light blue collar patches and cuff flaps edged with yellow lace; the epaulettes have light blue straps and fringes with yellow worsted crescents. His sky-blue trousers have double white seam stripes. He carries an M1842 musket, and is equipped with a black leather waist belt fastened with a rectangular gilt plate bearing the letters "BCG," supporting a black leather cap pouch. His cartridge box is slung from a black leather shoulder belt, and a militia knapsack is supported by black leather straps.

The enlisted man at left wears the "Class D" undress uniform of the **Maryland Guard Battalion, 53rd Maryland Volunteer Militia (G2)** – full dress headgear (see G3 & G4), a dark blue jacket trimmed with medium blue cord, and plain dark blue trousers with straight legs. His accoutrements consist of a black leather waist belt with 1860 oval brass plate bearing the state arms, supporting a black leather cartridge box and cap pouch.

His comrades display the full dress of the **Maryland Guard Battalion (G3 & G4)** – "Class A" chasseur uniform, consisting of a sky-blue chasseur-pattern cap with dark blue band and narrow yellow cord trim; a midnight-blue wool zouave jacket trimmed with yellow braid; and matching chasseur-pattern trousers with narrow yellow braid stripes and looped side pocket decoration, confined in white canvas gaiters. Under this is worn a medium-blue flannel pullover vest with red trim around the collar, and small brass ball buttons down the front between double rows of yellow lace. The weapon is the M1855 rifle-musket; a whitened buff leather waist belt with plain rectangular brass plate, worn over a deep red sash, supports a socket bayonet by a matching frog, and on the right rear a black leather cartridge box. The National Guard pattern rigid box knapsack, of black-painted canvas over wooden frames, has a messtin strapped to, and the number "53" painted on, the flap. The sky-blue wool blanket roll is embellished in red with the letters "MG."

H: MARYLAND INFANTRY, 1861–62

The colonel, **1st Maryland Infantry (H1)** is based on a photograph of Bradley T. Johnson. He waves a black felt "Hardee" hat with tall crown and yellow worsted braid and tassels. Rank insignia of three gold embroidered stars are displayed on the collar, and as three rows of gold braid knots on the forearms of his light gray shell jacket. His cadet-gray pants have gold seam stripes, and he wears high-cut black leather boots with spurs. He carries an M1850 Foot Officer's sword, and has a holstered revolver (hidden at this angle) attached to his black leather waist belt with two-piece Maryland state seal plate. A tooled leather haversack is slung over his right shoulder, while a narrower strap over the opposite shoulder supports a binocular case.

The enlisted man of **Co A, 2nd Battalion Maryland Infantry (H2)**, wears a small dark gray brimmed hat with black ostrich feather, a cadet-gray shell jacket with a plain low standing collar, and matching trousers. Thought to be an insignia of the "Maryland Line," a small gilt Maryland Cross is pinned to his left breast. He grips an M1842 musket in his gauntleted hands. A brown leather waist belt, fastened with an English "snake" clasp, supports a black leather cap pouch and a socket bayonet in a brown leather scabbard. A homemade blanket roll has replaced his earlier issue knapsack.

The uniform of the corporal, **Co I, 1st Maryland Volunteer Infantry (H3)**, includes a light gray "Corsican" cap with black band. The cadet-gray shell jacket has black tape trim around the top and bottom of the standing collar and the edges of the shoulder straps, and plain cuffs without buttons; his rank is indicated by two narrow black points-down chevrons, just visible here on the right upper sleeve only. Matching trousers have narrow black seam stripes. He is loading an M1816 flintlock musket converted to percussion; the black leather waist belt supports a cap pouch and a scabbarded socket bayonet, and is fastened with a Maryland militia oval plate. His cartridge box is slung from a black leather shoulder belt, and a tin canteen hangs from a white cotton sling.

Two corporals of the prewar Maryland Guard Battalion – see Plates G3 & G4. John Eager Howard Post (left) enlisted as a private in the 1st Maryland Infantry and was later commissioned a lieutenant in the 1st Maryland Cavalry. Charles R. Thompson (right) served as a private in the same cavalry regiment. Both men wear the "Class A" full dress chasseur uniform of the Maryland Guard Battalion, and Thompson holds an M1840 musician's sword. The numerals "53" on the rigid militia knapsack denote the number of the regiment to which this battalion was attached. The letters "M G" are just visible on the blue blanket roll. (Dave Mark Collection)

INDEX